The Worst Thing We've Ever Done

The Worst Thing We've Ever Done

ONE JUROR'S RECKONING WITH RACIAL INJUSTICE

Carol Menaker

SHE WRITES PRESS

Published 2023
Printed in the United States of America
Print ISBN: 978-1-64742-460-2
E-ISBN: 978-1-64742-461-9
Library of Congress Control Number: 2022912266

For information, address:
She Writes Press
1569 Solano Ave #546
Berkeley, CA 94707

She Writes Press is a division of SparkPoint Studio, LLC.

Names and identifying characteristics have been changed to protect the privacy of certain individuals.

For Frederick Muhammed Burton

Not everything that is faced can be changed;
but nothing can be changed until it is faced.
—James Baldwin

1

Six Days

For six days in June of 1976, in a spartan Philadelphia courtroom, African American prison inmate Freddy Burton was standing trial for the murders of two white prison wardens. Dressed in an ill-fitting sports jacket suitable for a funeral, Freddy sat nearly motionless in the stiff wooden chair at the long defense table. His dark face lit only by the harsh glare of the courtroom's fluorescent lights. His soft hands clasped as if in prayer on the table in front of him. I don't recall him ever speaking. To anyone.

For those same days, I sat in another stiff wooden chair in the jury box with eleven others. The twelve of us were there to decide Freddy Burton's fate.

As each witness placed a hand on a Bible and told his truth about what happened the day the wardens were massacred, I was watching Freddy Burton's face. His somber eyes and lifeless lips. I was watching for a sign, any sign, that he may not have done the horrible things he was accused of. Looking for clues that would tell me how in the world young Freddy Burton got himself into so much trouble. If the clues were there, I didn't see them. I couldn't see them.

Maybe it was because I was only twenty-four years old. Or maybe it was because I was white and privileged.

II

Summoned

The January air is crisp. The sun bright. The sky pristine and cloudless. A color blue I've only seen in California. From a drone overhead, the ground below must look like slithering snakes with fluttering pink scales inching forward in every direction along the side streets of the Capitol Mall. The pink scales are actually the heads of thousands of pink pussy-hatted men, women, and children bobbing along as they walk toward the Sacramento State Capitol on Tenth Street.

On the ground, the mood is county-fair festive. But there is no midway with corn dogs or sticky cotton candy or deep-fried Oreos. And there are no spinning Ferris wheels or 4-H teens tending their blue-ribbon pigs and goats. Instead, sprouting among the pink pussy-hatted heads are thousands of handmade protest signs in every size, shape, and color, announcing to the world why we are here.

It's 2017. My partner, Jerry, and I have driven the sixty miles to California's State Capitol to exorcise the insurmountable shock we feel at the election of Donald Trump. I, in particular, am here to also share my indignation that America missed its first real chance to send a woman to the White House. The dense like-minded crowd is close and comforting. Like one giant family.

Three nights ago, I was putting the finishing touches on my own pink hat with tiny ears. I hadn't looped a soft strand of yarn over a pair of knitting needles in more than five decades. The click of the metal kept the same steady rhythm that my mother's needles had long ago as she showed me how to move the yarn front to back to make even columns of stitches. Then, I had used remnants of navy and red yarn from a classic 1960s tennis sweater my oldest sister knitted years before. This time, I carefully chose a heathered pink from the few remaining pink skeins on the shelves of the local craft store. I was lost in those stitches—yarn in back, knit two; yarn in front, purl two; yarn in back, knit two; yarn in front, purl two. Counting the stitches was a gentle meditation that took my mind, at least for a few minutes, off the helplessness I'd been feeling since the night last November when the presidential election results came in. It was late when I got home from a choir rehearsal to find Jerry and his daughter Emily somber faced in front of the television.

"What's up?"

Their two heads shook "no" in unison.

"What's up?" I said louder. "Trump won? You're kidding, right?"

Their two heads shook in unison again. Emily was the one with the courage to speak.

"Yes, he won."

The two of them just sat there, numbed by the droning of the news. I turned away, walked upstairs to my bedroom, closed the door, and sat on the floor at the foot of the bed, hugging myself.

Now, we are at the Women's March in Sacramento to share our grief. The last time I marched with so many others was in 1970. I was a young freshman at Penn State when Ohio National Guardsmen opened fire on peaceful Vietnam War protestors at a university campus in Kent, Ohio. I have been haunted ever since by the *Life* magazine photo of Mary Ann Vecchio kneeling over the lifeless body of Jeffrey Miller. Jeffrey was one of four students senselessly killed that day. Nine others were wounded. It was another scary time.

But now I am here where the collective energy of tens of thousands of hearts beating in rhythm and that many voices shouting in unison is staggering. "What do we want? Justice. When do we want it? Now."

As I let the waves of chanting roll over me, I want to hug each and every pink-hatted creature here. Thanks to them, the piano-wire-tight feeling in my chest eases just enough so I can take a deep breath. At least for these few hours, everyone here believes our voices will be heard.

It's nearly 5:00 p.m. when we pull up in front of our gingerbread-trimmed Victorian. I'm still high from the day's rally. It feels good to be out of the darkness and into hope. Jerry takes the ritual walk across the street to our rural mailbox. I grab our day packs from the back of the minivan and head to the porch, thinking about what to make for dinner. I'm hungry.

"Any mail for me?"

"Mm-hmm, yeah, but you're not going to like it."

"Is it my credit card bill?"

"Nope."

I cringe. "Okay. Is it the electric bill?" The monthly electric bill with the month-to-month, year-to-year bar charts of our usage was always a source of contention between Jerry and me. In his mind, there was a direct correlation between the charges, whatever they were, and the degree to which we failed to conserve. We just didn't seem to be able to agree on how green was green enough. Though I hesitated to be direct about it, I resented the idea of giving up my modest needs for personal comfort to be any greener than I was.

"Nope, not the electric bill."

"Then it has to be the IRS."

"Nope."

As I set our bags on the floor inside the front door, he handed me a midsize self-mailer. The return address was the Nevada County Superior Court. Printed within a red stripe across the middle of the mailer in oversize, bold capital letters were two words: JURY SUMMONS.

"Fuck!"

Every jury summons that arrived in the mail in every county in every state I lived in from West Virginia to Florida to Illinois to the great state of California was like a spot fire on a grassy hillside. There was no single piece of mail that triggered more dread, and Jerry knew this.

With the arrival of each summons, the innate instincts of fight or flight exploded in my chest. There had to be a way out. And since I hated any kind of confrontation, it would have to be flight. I will say with little compunction that I would lie, cheat, or steal to get out of this particular civic responsibility. Well, I wouldn't cheat or steal. But I would lie. Outrageous, opinionated, far-from-the-truth answers about biases I have against law enforcement and those who break the law. Or maybe it would be better to just stand up and tell the judge it simply wasn't possible for me to serve. "Your Honor," I would say, "I believe I met my lifetime commitment to jury service in 1976 when I was sequestered for twenty-one days in the trial of a bloody double homicide inside one of Pennsylvania's most infamous prisons. Two white wardens dead. Two Black inmates convicted of murder. Forgive me, Your Honor, if this sounds unpatriotic, but I have no intention of anteing up again."

III
Flight

The small ten-by-twelve-foot dining room in our house is the hub of our lives in the Sierra Foothills of California. Jerry and I sit across from each other and each of us "owns" our side of the smooth cherrywood dining table that Jerry built more than thirty years ago. The piles on my side are generally in neat stacks: unpaid bills, unread catalogs, often a book or two and a seven-day pill organizer I thought only old people used. When my stacks get too high, I move them from the table to the empty chair next to me, where my backpack and hat hang off the back corner. These days I need as much space to breathe as I can get.

Jerry would be lying if he said he has less stuff on his side of the table than I do on mine. Not that it matters. But he has folders with records of his doctor visits from the last I-don't-know-how-many years, at least six pens—you can never have too many pens—recycled calendar pages for notetaking, a whole raft of daily reminder notes about things he needs to remember, and two little books with his computer logins and passwords, both of which routinely fail him when he tries to access his online accounts. When his pile gets too big, he moves it somewhere else and starts over.

I'm not fond of his dependence on these miscellaneous colored

Post-it Notes. It only reminds me that he can't remember as much as I can, which leaves me in the unwelcome position of remembering all the details of both of our lives.

We eat most of our meals at this table. At breakfast over a healthy bowl of oatmeal with fruit and nuts and steaming cups of coffee, we orient ourselves to the day. Jerry reads the newspaper or newspapers online. I check my email and get the day's look at pictures of Jackson, my grandson who lives in too hot, too far away South Florida—three thousand miles from Northern California.

On this particular morning, I feel smothered by the detritus of our lives. I'm still troubled by yesterday's ominous arrival of the jury summons. *You're not a kid anymore*, I tell myself. *This is a no-brainer. Just put it on your calendar and do it. Besides, what are the odds that there will be a murder case in rural Nevada County, California, population less than one hundred thousand? Or that I will, for the second time in my life, have the misfortune of winning the juror lottery?*

There was the possibility of rescheduling if I had a conflict on my calendar. You got one shot at that according to the information on the summons. A few quick keystrokes to my calendar nixed that. Other than my regular yoga class and the Tuesday-morning ride with the local cycling group, nada. I feel momentarily embarrassed at how little purpose there is to my life since I retired.

"I wonder if there's someplace online I can check the calendar of hearings," I say out loud and half to myself. I am in dire need of moral support if I have to face jury duty again alone. "Huh," Jerry murmurs without ever taking his eyes off the latest copy of the AARP magazine.

"There must be a public calendar of the scheduled hearings at the courthouse," I say, slower and louder. "I need to see what's scheduled for the date of my summons. You know they still call jurors even if there are no scheduled hearings. That's when you get the real pass."

"Mm-hmm."

I know better than to try to divert Jerry's attention from the morning newspaper. Though a lot is shared in the hour or so before we activate our daily schedules, little is retained, unless of course it's written on a Post-it to-do list.

"Never mind." This time I am muttering to myself. I start pecking through the county courthouse website to find a listing of the trials. "Fuck! You are not going to believe this!" This time I am not talking to myself. "The week of my summons there is actually a murder trial. It's from a murder a few years ago. Some guy in Truckee killed his girlfriend and threw her body over the Rainbow Bridge in Tahoe. Holy crap!"

"What?" This is an absentminded, disinterested *what* that says, *I think I'm supposed to be listening, but I have no idea what she's ranting about.*

I slow my words and turn up the volume so they will register. "The week of my summons there is a murder trial on the schedule. That settles it. I'm going to take my one chance at a get-out-of-jail-free card and at least reschedule. One murder trial in a lifetime is enough."

Resolute, I complete the request form for rescheduling, refold the summons mailer, carefully attach an American Flag Forever stamp right side up, and walk it to the mailbox for the carrier to pick up on his daily route. Flag up. Done.

It turns out to be a busier day than most. We have invited friends for dinner and there is shopping to do, and we must create some order out of the piled-high dining room table so that six people can sit at it and enjoy an uncluttered meal. Ahh.

—

The stories I tell about my jury service have never included the grit of the murders or the life sentence without parole the judge handed down to the defendant. Instead, it is the experience of the sequestration that feeds the narrative. The tedious food at the hotel restaurant. The twelve of us marching in formation to and from the courthouse and on field trips. Yes, field trips. Then there was Cheryl Ann Russo, juror #3, from Philly's Fishtown neighborhood. No day of that dreadful sequestration went by without Mrs. Russo tearfully telling the saga of her homemade pasta sauce. The large cans of San Marzano tomatoes she bought on sale at the Acme. The garlic and onions and fresh basil and oregano. Cheryl wept her way through each step of her preparation. Sauté the onions and garlic, smash the San Marzanos with the back of a wooden spoon, then simmer it for hours with handfuls of fresh basil and oregano. All to make the perfect marinara for her husband, who, she told us, would starve to death without her home cooking.

I don't talk about the defense attorney's braggadocio, or his slimy half-smoked cigar balanced on the low wall between the defense table and the observers. I don't talk about the Oscar-worthy testimony of the defendant's fellow inmate who shamelessly pronounced that he alone stabbed the two wardens to death. And I don't talk about the fear and frustration I felt every single one of the days I was sequestered.

Jerry can testify that I've mastered the telling of those stories. For him, it's like a television rerun. He knows the story and most of the punchlines and just where an audience of dinner guests is likely to laugh.

Given the arrival of my summons, it was no surprise that the subject of jury duty was top of mind when the dinner guests arrived.

As we lingered over my own homemade lasagna and sipped decent red wine, I told my stories and got my laughs. At the end of the evening, our guests left with full stomachs and high spirits.

Jerry was at the sink sloshing soapy water around in the pasta pot while I picked through a steep pile of plastic deli containers for the leftover lasagna. As I snapped the lid onto a container, I realized something that hadn't occurred to me for all the years I'd been telling my jury duty story.

"When I tell those stories about what it was like to be on that jury, how come no one ever asks about the guy who went to prison?"

"I dunno. It's always seemed like the story was about you."

I gave him a squeeze around the waist before he could hand me the dripping-wet pot to dry. "That's really bad, isn't it? That I never talk about him. I have no idea what his story was. He never testified. I guess he's still in jail somewhere. Or maybe he's dead. That was a long time ago."

It's 3:00 a.m. Our spoiled cat, Lucy, has suctioned all her thirteen pounds to the space at the foot of our bed. I can't move my feet without disturbing her, and I know she has no intention of moving from whatever dreamland she's in. My mind is racing. I'm thinking about that question I asked Jerry over the soapy lasagna pot. Why hasn't anyone ever asked about Freddy Burton when I tell my jury duty story? In all these years, I haven't spent a single minute wondering who Freddy Burton was before he was arrested, indicted, and convicted of murder.

I try to imagine the house he grew up in. Was it a duplex on a tree-lined street like the house I grew up in or an apartment in Philadelphia's low-income housing? Was he in his high school plays like I was or did he play forward on a winning basketball team? Or both? What about his family? His mother? Did he have sisters or brothers? Aunts or uncles or cousins? I imagine his extended family at a grand Thanksgiving dinner passing the buttery mashed potatoes, the turkey with stuffing, and the tray of sweet Ocean Spray cranberry sauce sliced into perfect round ruby disks, just like we did. Did his family cry for him when he got in trouble? Were they still crying for him?

I make it a habit to take early morning walks along the trails near our house before the sun has a chance to burn off the morning dew. I especially love those few weeks between spring and summer when the feather-leafed cedars and mountain maples cast lacework shadows on the road before me and the resident red-shouldered hawk squawks loudly as it takes off overhead into the woods. From below the road, I can hear the rushing of mountain-water-fed Deer Creek, where 150 years ago thousands of miners swarmed the landscape laying claim to California's gold near American Hill and Lost Hill and Champion Mines. Now all those places are neighborhoods where people live twenty-first-century lives.

Today my pace is sluggish though. I'm tired from a sleepless night. As I walk alone between the filigree of shade and the bright sun on the open trail, I'm still thinking about Freddy Burton. About who I was so long ago. About who I'd become. About who he might have become if things had worked out differently. As I pick up my pace, the crunchy gravel is spinning out from under my feet. In the middle of all this natural beauty, a burning sensation rises in my chest. "You think you're so damned smart! Well, if you're so smart . . . if you're so smart," I shout to the ridge of the trees in the cloudless sky, "why didn't you know more?"

I'm desperate, and I pick up my pace to get home where I can google Frederick Burton.

—

It takes me all of three seconds to type the fifteen characters of his name into my search engine. The search rolls out more Frederick Burtons than I want to count: an American actor, a real estate agent in Fort Lauderdale, a nineteenth-century Irish painter named Sir Frederic Burton, without a *k*. There are Frederick Burtons in Manchester, New Hampshire; Houston, Texas; and Myrtle Beach, South Carolina. I keep scrolling. On the third page of results between two separate entries for a Dr. Frederick Burton in Macon, Georgia, is a PDF of a court document dated September 26, 2013. It is a petition to the United States District Court for the Eastern District of Pennsylvania for a writ of habeas corpus. The petition was denied. The plaintiff was Frederick Burton. On the next half-dozen pages of search results there are other petitions over several years. Most of them have to do with legal challenges to Freddy's first conviction in 1972 for the murder of Fairmount Park police officer Francis Von Colln. This is the conviction that landed him in prison in the first place. The petitions claim that the testimony of a key witness in that trial had been coerced by the police. In exchange for her testimony against Freddy, the petitions cited, the witness was given immunity from prosecution as a coconspirator and Freddy went to jail with a life sentence.

Maybe he shouldn't have been in jail in the first place. If he'd been acquitted of that crime, he wouldn't have even been in prison—and certainly not in the warden's office—a year later when the two wardens were slain.

More troubling though was a petition for a new trial in the prison murders. The petition claimed that Freddy's attorney was inebriated during the proceedings and unable to give good counsel. Holy crap! I am instantly transported back to the courtroom. To memories of what felt like his attorney bullying the witnesses. I now have to wonder if his lawyer's courtroom theatrics were really just the effect of being two—or even three—sheets to the wind.

I'm feeling sickened by what I see. Something had gone terribly wrong for Freddy Burton. Not only in the apocryphal six days of the prison-murder trial I served on as a juror, but in the six years before that, when he was arrested for the Von Colln murder. Since 1970 Freddy had filed four Post-Conviction Relief Act petitions and three federal habeases. Each and every one of them was dismissed on procedural grounds. He'd never been given a chance to make a substantive argument about his trials or the justice he believed he was denied.

As I sift through link after link, the memories I stored away from 1976 start taking on subtle shades of gray. What I was certain of in 1976, I am not certain of now.

My heart goes out to Freddy Burton, and my mind is doing everything it can to catch up with it. For reasons I can't explain, a certain resolve comes over me. Maybe it's because it's looking like Freddy Burton may have been wrongly convicted—twice. That maybe he'd unjustly spent almost fifty years in prison instead of growing old with his children and grandchildren. Maybe it's because I know that if I was part of such a travesty of justice, I need to make it right. It all seems to come down to that. Doing the right thing, whatever that is. To do that, I need to know more. The older, wiser human being in me needs to know more.

Among the links to Frederick Burton whirring around cyberspace is one with a simple heading: "Free Frederick Burton." I see that it was posted by Jonathan Gettleman, a white civil rights attorney in Santa Cruz, California, only two hundred miles from my front door and three thousand miles away from the Keystone State of

Pennsylvania. From his photo, I peg him in his early forties. There is also a photo of Freddy in an orange prison jumpsuit. He is not alone in the picture. I don't know who the others are. This is the first website in the pages of search results I've found that confirms that Freddy is alive and still racking up the years of his sentences in a Pennsylvania prison.

Like the petitions that surfaced online, Jonathan Gettleman's posting claims that Freddy's 1972 conviction of the Von Colln murder was unfair. That the Philadelphia District Attorney's office had obstructed justice and turned a blind eye to the perjury of the only witness to testify against Freddy.

But there is one important question that is left unanswered in Mr. Gettleman's narrative. Nowhere is there a mention of Freddy's conviction in the prison murders. Let's say Gettleman is right. Let's say he is successful at getting a hearing and that Freddy's 1972 conviction is overturned. How does Freddy become free with a second conviction for the prison murders? With Gettleman so close, it's hard to resist reaching out to him. But I don't. Not right then. It's all too unsettling.

Jerry pushes back when I tell him about Gettleman's claims and Freddy still being alive in prison.

"Let it go," he tells me. "People in prison have networks on the outside, you know. I don't think it's the best idea to keep digging into this. What exactly are you trying to get at anyway? You did the best you could at the time with the information you had. Just let it go."

In his defense, Jerry is just being protective. He's worried that I might be stepping into a dangerous world. But I'm not biting.

"He's in jail in Pennsylvania," I fire back. "Exactly how would that work? Like he's going to send a hit man to California because some old lady is looking into the murders? I don't think so." Then I say out loud words that haven't crossed my mind since I served on that jury more than forty years before. "Besides, I'm not sure Freddy actually murdered someone. I'm not sure he murdered anyone."

IV

Juror #4

It was 1976 and the City of Philadelphia was just a month away from celebrating the nation's two hundredth year of independence. Bicentennial fever was wildly infectious. Puppet shows and street theater and concerts were springing up in neighborhoods across the city. Thousands of street banners showcased the red, white, and blue bicentennial insignia. Even the city's fire hydrants took on patriotic colors, and millions of tourists were making the pilgrimage to Independence Hall to pay homage to the Liberty Bell.

Until that moment, I was poised on the launching pad of a perfect 1970s life. The life that would blend seamlessly with my postwar 1950s childhood and my 1960s baby boomer teen years. In 1969, the year I graduated from William Penn High School, Neil Armstrong stepped onto the powdery surface of the moon. "One small step for man, one giant leap for mankind," he said. Anything was possible.

Seven years later, I was a twenty-four-year-old married college grad running off newsletters on the mimeograph machine at a nonprofit led by some of Philadelphia's most liberal and prominent movers and shakers. We were going to turn around the city's public schools. Make them accountable. Being a part of that felt honorable and right.

Until that moment, I lived my life for the future. For when my husband, Mark, and I had a family and for when we bought our rented two-story row house on Twenty-Sixth Street to make our own. Everything was possible, and I had it all.

But with all the city's bicentennial pomp and circumstance and amid the vast landscape of hope I lived in, I found myself on the fourteenth floor of Philadelphia's Center City Holiday Inn sitting on the lid of the porcelain commode and silently counting the four-inch-square ceramic tiles that lined the walls of the bathroom's shower. There were 486 tiles. From that I calculated a total of 7,776 square inches. Or fifty-four square feet of white ceramic tile.

I was alone in that hotel room. The TV remote didn't work. There was no dial tone on the bedside-table telephone. No room service. There was only me, at twenty-four years old, in the last place I wanted to be.

I can't know what occupied the others in rooms along the hallway outside my door. They too may have been counting tiles. Or lying back on their faded chenille bedspreads staring at the ceiling. Or maybe they were looking out the picture window at the living street fourteen stories below. Or maybe, just maybe, as I was doing, they were considering daisy-chaining the top and bottom bedsheets from the two double beds, climbing out the window, and rappelling down the outside of the building. I remember thinking about that James Bond-style escape a lot. But I worried that if I miscalculated, I might end up one full story short of the street. Caught midair, swinging. Too far to drop and too far to climb back up. If I lost my grip, I'd be badly injured, if not killed, in the fall. If I survived, attempting to escape sequestered jury duty would be, to say the least, frowned on and would most likely end with my being charged with contempt of court.

I was juror #4. I couldn't have known it would be fifteen more days separated from the world I knew before the complement of eleven jurors took up residence with me and the trial would begin.

The day before, I was one of hundreds called for a *voir dire* where prospective jurors were questioned by prosecuting and defense attorneys to determine their fitness to serve. Small groups at a time were led into Judge Lawrence Prattis's wood-paneled courtroom in Philadelphia's ornate, sculpture-laden city hall building at Broad and Market Streets.

The defendant Frederick Burton, a young Black man, was one of two inmates who were in the warden's office at Holmesburg Prison when the violent stabbings of two wardens—yes, two wardens—took place. The prison's captain of the guards was also assaulted. He survived.

The opposing attorneys took their places. Though I didn't know at the time how prominent each was, I can tell you now that each had his own pedigree. Cecil Moore, Freddy Burton's defense attorney, was an eminent African American lawyer who advocated for civil rights and at one time served as the president of the Philadelphia chapter of the NAACP. His street-brawler style, deep Southern accent, and penchant for cigars and alcohol contributed to a larger-than-life character in the courtroom.

In sharp contrast, Wilhelm "Bill" Knauer Jr., seemingly one of the district attorney's office's best and brightest, was a simple puritan. Knauer did however have his own pedigree as the second generation of a high-profile white family committed to public service. His father was the state's deputy attorney general. His mother was later appointed by President Ronald Reagan as the nation's first director of the Office of Consumer Affairs. Both Moore and Knauer were accustomed to winning. Given the high-profile nature of the crime, each of them had something to prove.

The 1973 murders of two white wardens by two Black inmates was a crime of biblical proportions. Newspapers reported the blood-spattered walls and flecks of dried blood on the floor of the warden's office. The eerie quiet in the prison's locked-down cellblocks. The rage of the city's mayor. The calls to reinstitute the state's death penalty. And the thousands who filled the city's church pews to mourn Wardens Curran and Fromhold. According to prison officials, the two wardens were the only city correctional officers to have died in the line of duty in modern times. And the weeks of news coverage of the slayings was so racially charged and polarizing that most of Philadelphia's citizenry had already taken sides. Many of those same Philadelphians knew about Freddy Burton's first conviction three years before—the murder of white police officer Francis Von Colln—the one that landed Freddy in prison in the first place.

Looking back on all this, as jurors go, I was the perfect catch. So perfect, I might as well have landed in the city hall courtyard in a hot air balloon from Kansas. I was new to the city, having lived there for only two years. I knew nothing of the prison murders and nothing of Freddy Burton's first conviction. I was young, white, and educated, and I appeared to be thoughtful and open-minded. And finally, I had the right answers to the two questions the two attorneys could agree on.

I've since been told that lawyers often choose jurors who are stupid. Those who will choose the simple path to a verdict. I prefer to think of myself at that time as unknowing.

"Ms. Michaels, do you believe everything a police officer says is true?" drawled Moore in an accent from somewhere hundreds of miles south of Philadelphia.

I remember pausing before answering, wondering if it was some sort of trick question. "No, not really."

Moore then strutted over to the defense table and put his hand on the defendant's shoulder. He spoke slowly as he asked, "Ms. Michaels, do you believe this man is guilty because he's Black?"

The question caught me so off guard I had to think about my answer. Was there somewhere the presumption that I should or might have thought this man was guilty just because he was Black?

I remember looking directly at the defendant. From where I was sitting in the witness box, I saw a young Black man of slight stature. He was wearing a dark sports jacket that hung loosely from his shoulders. I don't remember if he wore a tie or not. I do remember his hair. It was picked out in a soft, uneven Afro. And his eyes, I remember them as somber. I focused my eyes back on the lawyer and answered his question firmly: "No, I don't. I don't believe he's guilty because he's Black."

In quick lockstep, the two attorneys approached the judge's bench. I watched them as they exchanged a few words with the judge then stepped back from the bench to take their seats.

"Mrs. Michaels," the judge said, "You're to go with the court officer. We'll contact your husband to get your things."

We'd been told that this trial would require sequestration. I knew in theory what that meant, but I wasn't prepared for the immediate nature of being cut off from the world I knew. *We'll contact your husband to get your things.* The judge's words spun inside my head. Just hours before I had walked from my downtown office to city hall for what I thought was nothing more than an afternoon commitment to jury service. I was running late and didn't have time for lunch, so I stopped by the soft-pretzel vendor at Twelfth and Chestnut for a salty, doughy pretzel with just the right amount of yellow mustard—not so much that it would drip on my new pantsuit. Pretzel in hand as I walked, I eyed the stylish mannequins in John Wanamaker's department store windows and reminded myself that I needed to choose a gift for my sister in Mississippi, whose birthday was only a week away. It was one of those mid-May East Coast days when the temperature boosts upward of eighty-five degrees, a preview of the steamy summer to come. I remember wishing that I'd left my new linen jacket hanging over the back of my office chair.

We'll contact your husband to get your things. The blood rushed from my head and the low hum of background noise inside my ears gave me the horrible sensation that I might faint. I gripped the arms of the witness stand's hard wooden chair and told myself to breathe. I wasn't sure what scared me more: being sequestered or fainting in front of a courtroom full of people I didn't know and didn't care to know. When the chill of panic dropped from my chest to my stomach, I desperately hoped I wouldn't throw up. It was suddenly so cold in that courtroom. I remember thinking it was a good thing I didn't leave my jacket behind. I don't know why I felt so frightened, but my teeth were chattering, and my body was trembling inside and out.

A matronly uniformed court officer stepped toward me and waited as I walked down the three steps to the main courtroom floor. From there, I was escorted to a conference room just outside. I was to wait there, I was told, until the jury selection for the day was completed. Then I and any others who were selected for service would be taken to a local hotel for the duration of the jury selection and trial. In this particular case, the sequestration would be complete, the officer told me. No contact with family or others unless through a court officer. Access to only minimal personal items. No access to news or other written material that might influence someone's thinking about the case.

"How long will all this go on?" I asked the court officer, hoping my voice wasn't shaking like the rest of me.

"Hard to say, hon'. But it could be a while. Can I get you anything before I leave? Something to drink? A Coke maybe?"

I let my weight sink into the cold flat of the chair, folded my hands in my lap, and breathed again. "I'm okay. Thanks." I was grateful for her small kindness.

Alone in that room, my mind bounced back to Freddy Burton's eyes. How gentle they were. I could almost say repentant. Not the eyes of someone who could commit murder. But whoever this guy was, he must have committed one heck of a crime to be in prison in the first place. People who were in prison were there for good reason. I knew that for certain. Had he killed someone or raped someone? I had no clue. And then to murder two prison wardens? How in the world could that happen inside a maximum-security prison?

The room was silent and airless. I wondered if it was soundproof. A large round government-issue clock hung high on the wall above the door. And a water cooler with a stack of white paper cone cups balanced on top was set back in one far corner. Above the cooler to the left was a simply framed eight-by-ten-inch black-and-white photo of Mayor Frank Rizzo of Philadelphia. To Rizzo's left was a photo of Gerald Ford of the same size. President Ford's photo was in color.

Breathe.

I pulled the linen jacket of my pantsuit tight and berated myself for choosing to wear that particular outfit on that particular day. The jacket and pants were already halfway to being so wrinkled it looked like I'd slept in them. *That's what you get with linen*, I chastised myself. It wasn't the first time I'd been swayed by the crisp, untouched look of linen on a store-window mannequin, and the color of this was—well, a lovely coral. Then I noticed my fingernails and wished I'd clipped them. There was no telling how long it would be before I could get my hands on a pair of fingernail clippers.

Breathe. Chatter. Breathe. Chatter. Breathe. Chatter. Chatter.

Would my husband, Mark, know to put the hamburger that was thawing on the counter back in the refrigerator? Would he remember to feed the cats and scoop the kitty litter? To take in the mail? My Toyota was in the shop for an oil change. Would Mark know to pick it up? Who would cancel my eye doctor appointment tomorrow?

Breathe. I pulled a deep breath into my chest and let it go.

In the near silence, the only sound was the even *tick, tick, tick* of the wall clock. It was 3:00. I stopped fretting for a moment and watched the black second hand take tiny purposeful jumps from one short black mark to the next, just as it had when I was waiting for the bell to ring at the end of school in the third grade. Some days that ticking was endless. I thought 3:30 would never come.

Then I looked at the door and felt myself drop down to the next level of panic. Jeeesus! What if the door was locked? What if I needed something? What if I got a migraine? I got up and walked to the door and put my hand on the brass knob and just held it there.

What I wanted, more than anything I'd ever wanted, was to walk back into that courtroom, interrupt the proceedings, and tell all assembled that they'd made a terrible mistake. That I should not be locked alone in this tomb of an office waiting for juror #5 or #6 or #7. That I could never be an unbiased juror. That all I knew about being Black and in prison, not to mention murder, was that it wasn't a good thing. I'd tell the judge the only Black people I ever knew were my mother's housekeepers. I'd tell him that as a young child I was so naive about race that I wondered if the brown skin I saw on colored people was also brown on the parts of their bodies I couldn't see under their clothes. I'd tell the Black Southern lawyer that I was fifteen years old before I attended an integrated public school and that even then, most of the Black kids were either in the vo-tech or special-ed sections. Not in the pre-college section like me.

I'd tell him how alarm bells went off when the first young man to ask me out in college was Black and that I made up an excuse not to go out with him. I'd tell the white prep-school prosecutor that I'd seen enough cop shows on TV to know, truthfully, that you can't always believe what a policeman says. And finally, I'd tell them all that I had a life and that I would much prefer to live it exactly as I had anticipated living it when my alarm clock went off at 7:30 this morning.

Breathe.

Then my fingers loosened their grip on the doorknob. I turned back to the chair, sat down, straightened my wrinkled jacket, and tucked my purse close between my hip and the chair's wooden spindles. I never turned the knob. I didn't want to know just how stuck I might have been.

I felt nine years old again, away from home for the first time at Camp Rockhill in Quakertown, just over eighty miles from my hometown in Harrisburg, Pennsylvania. I'd been at camp less than a week and I was desperately homesick. In spite of my pleading over the phone to be picked up, my parents didn't come for me.

"Give it time," my mother said.

I can't tell you how long I sat there waiting for juror #5, passing time, listening to the relentless ticking of that clock. I can't tell you if I walked the three blocks from city hall to the Center City Holiday Inn in tandem with a court officer or if I was ducked into a city vehicle, driven up Broad Street to Thirteenth, and delivered to the hotel's front door, where bellhops were attending to paying guests and carting overfilled dollies of luggage through the lobby's glass doors. I can't tell you if I was somehow registered at the front desk or if there was just a nod from a court officer to the hotel clerk as the officer and I unceremoniously boarded the elevator, where she pressed the button for the fourteenth floor.

The first real memory I have of the hotel was being shown to my room. Just inside the door was my small tan-and-black tweed overnight bag. Mark must have brought it when he got the call from a court officer. The bag's small size was comforting. Maybe he knew my stay wouldn't be long. The female court officer stepped by me in the doorway, glanced around the room, opened and closed the closet and bathroom doors, and looked behind the blackout curtains. Then she turned to leave, handing me my room key.

"We'll be meeting at the elevator at 5:30 to go down for dinner. Please be ready on time. You won't want to keep the others waiting."

It was 5:00 in the afternoon. There was no juror #5 that day. I sat down on the bed and unzipped the small bag. Its contents were barely enough to settle in for the night and only one change of underwear. It crossed my mind that if I didn't sort that out somehow between Mark and my captors, I'd be washing my underwear out in the sink and wearing that same wrinkled linen pantsuit for days.

I was hoping for something other than overnight necessities in that bag. Something special, some surprise from Mark. We used to call them "*S*'s"—for surprises, that is. A small item that only the two of us had shared to show he was thinking about me and wishing I was home. This would be the first time we'd slept in separate beds since our wedding night. What could have been more romantic and loving than a special "*S*," tucked away inside that tweedy bag?

I turned every pocket of that bag inside out. Nada. Defeated, I took the TV remote to look for the evening news. Again nada. I picked up the phone to call the front desk about the errant television.

Nada again. Then I laid back on the pillows and closed my eyes. That cheap tweed overnight bag was my only connection to the real world.

In the spirit of cooperation, I did what was asked and met an entourage at the elevator at 5:30. A Black man in his mid-fifties, a Black woman a bit younger, and an overweight middle-aged white woman with acne and bleached, permed hair stood together by the closed elevator door. They were flanked on two sides by uniformed court officers. Guessing they were jurors #1, #2, and #3, I took up my place with them, careful not to speak. I didn't know the rules. We took the first empty elevator down the fourteen floors, bypassing other elevator-button-pushing guests on the way down. In the dining room, we were shown to a long table set with ice water–filled goblets and starched white napkins in the shape of small crowns ruling over salad plates with wedges of iceberg lettuce doused in thick pink Russian dressing. The table was set for at least twenty. It seemed whoever had made the dinner arrangements was a bit optimistic about completing the selection of a jury of twelve plus two alternates in only one day.

Like a high school clique, the court officers peeled off from the group and took seats together at the far end of the table. Already bonding in some mysterious way, the three others who I believed to be jurors and I took seats together closer to the window overlooking a small outdoor courtyard.

The smells of the table linen's chalky laundry soap, grilled steak, some sort of fishy seafood, French onion soup, and reheated baked potatoes with sour cream and chives set my stomach on edge. I was supposed to have taken the evening 5:10 bus home and be having hamburgers for dinner and watching *60 Minutes* and *M*A*S*H* on TV with my husband. I wondered if the other jurors were as shell-shocked as I was. If they too were giving up some daily routine they counted on. Surely they were.

The Black man handed me his menu and introduced himself.

"I'm Willard, and you must be juror #4, the last juror of the day." He was smiling. Then, touching the shoulder of the Black woman next to him, he continued, "This is Alene, and this," he held his hand palm up toward the other woman, "is Cheryl Ann. And you are?"

"Carol."

"Well, Carol, it looks like we have all won the jackpot, doesn't it?"

Cheryl Ann was tucking a stiff napkin into the collar of her housedress. Her close-set eyes looked worried.

"The TV and phone in my room don't work," I reported to Willard. "I'll somehow need to get to the front desk about that."

"Oh, ours don't work either," Willard answered for himself and the others. "They've turned them off so we won't watch the news or talk to anyone outside about the case. There is one room down the hall upstairs with a TV if you want to watch it, but there's a lot of competition for what to watch. No news either way." Willard seemed to know the ropes. He must have been juror #1. I could only guess how long he'd been there.

When it was my turn to order, I closed the menu and asked for a cup of hot tea. Then I started building a mental wall around myself, withdrawing to somewhere inside where I could feel safe. I had no plans to make friends or break bread with these people for very long. I had no intention of completing my civic duty. All that mattered was when and how I was going to get myself out of that place.

V
Sequestered

The first night after dinner, we were shuttled up the elevators and safely installed back in our rooms. I walked around the room fingering the faux bamboo wallpaper, the chenille spread, and the smooth desktop. I eyed the blank screen on the television and the silent telephone and just for good measure once again tested the TV remote control. Nada. When I put the phone receiver to my ear, there was no dial tone. I was simply not ready to give up on those creature comforts. So much so that I continued to test the TV and the phone every single day of the twenty-one days I was sequestered. I was truly cut off from the outside world. Unless of course some renegade housekeeper or building manager could actually access these devices and turn them on without the knowledge of the court officers. Crazy thinking. But that's where my head was. There had to be someone out there on my side, and I chose to believe it was an errant empathetic hotel staff member who'd observed enough sequestered juries to step up and save the day.

Someone once suggested that sequestration wasn't all that bad. That three free square meals a day and a spic-and-span room without your kids underfoot or your boss giving you shit might be as pleasant as a vacation at the Jersey shore. Without, of course, the charm of briny-smelling seawater or the gritty sand that inevitably finds its way to the floor of your beachside apartment no matter how hard you try to wipe your feet in the outdoor corridor. Being on jury duty and having all one's needs met without effort was better than a stick in the eye, they said.

If there were those in the lockup with me who shared that belief, I didn't meet them. I was operating on the presumption that everyone there on the fourteenth floor of that three-out-of-five-star hotel, including the court officers, would have rather been home eating takeout pizza, pouring a glass of chardonnay, watching Carol Burnett wink at the audience and pull on her ear at the end of her weekly variety show, and sleeping in their own beds.

I somehow found my way to sleep that first night. Panic and exhaustion will do that to you.

As days passed, more jurors randomly joined the club. Some days, there were none, and other days, the group gained as many as two or more. I don't remember much of it. Most of what I remember is tedium and frustration and a healthy dose of anger. I couldn't stop asking myself what I'd done wrong in my life to deserve this.

Jury sequestration has a long history, with its roots in English common law. The reason juries are sequestered is to ensure that the defendant has a fair trial by restricting the jury's access to the media and members of the community, including their friends and family, who might influence their decision. But some have argued that sequestration can and does impact the frame of mind of at least some jurors. I can certainly attest to that.

In more recent history, jury sequestration has been a relatively uncommon practice, reserved only for the most high-profile cases. The decision to sequester a jury is up to the judge, who may choose to sequester during the trial, during deliberations, or both. But these days, and I'm guessing even in 1976, it is and was rare for members of a jury to be sequestered as soon as they are selected, before the trial begins, as well as during the trial and through deliberations. The fact that the jury I served on experienced that kind of full and complete sequestration testifies to the judge's view of the seriousness and public nature of the crime committed and the risk that the verdict could be influenced by factors outside the courtroom.

In 1970, it took five weeks, or twenty court days, for the jury in the famous Charles Manson case to be selected. Those jurors were sequestered immediately upon being sworn in, just as we were. In 1995, jurors in the O. J. Simpson trial were sequestered only from the beginning of the trial through deliberations. It was the longest jury sequestration in American history. An extraordinary and I suspect painful 265 days.

In the Derek Chauvin trial for the murder of George Floyd, jurors were "partially sequestered" for four weeks, in which they were escorted by members of the Hennepin County Sheriff's Office as a group through a private entrance to the courthouse and supervised in the courthouse during the trial. They were permitted to go home at night and then were fully sequestered only for the ten hours over the two days of deliberations.

It should be noted that sequestering a jury is also costly. The expense of hotel rooms, meals, field trips, and overtime pay for court officers, multiplied by twenty-one, the number of days I was sequestered, must have added up to tens of thousands of dollars. It's been reported that the cost to sequester the O. J. Simpson jury was nearly $2 million.

More than forty years later, I can't tell you why I didn't just run for it. Was there a court officer stationed at the elevator and at the emergency exit stairwell? All things considered, I don't think I looked for an emergency exit. I probably should have known where that exit was. Why didn't I just run? Maybe it was a sense of obligation I had. That damned obligation to do the right thing, even in the face of misery. I guess when we look closely enough, we're surprised by what we see in ourselves.

After the first night, a pattern was established at bedtime. A gentle knock on my door announced a court officer, who then delivered the nightly phone message from my husband. "Mrs. Michaels," she whispered loudly enough to be heard through the door. "Your husband called, he says he loves you." I never replied to her. If her words were intended to be soothing, they weren't. She didn't know Mark. She didn't know me. Besides, if Mark really loved me, he'd find a way to get me out of there.

Bedtime was when I missed my life the most. To find comfort, I settled in, plumped and piled the pillows from both beds against the headboard, sat back against them, closed my eyes, and let my mind wander to another time and place.

Just the week before, Mark and I were snuggling thigh to thigh on our Haitian cotton sofa, his arm draped around my shoulders. We were looking through our wedding album. It was nearly dusk outside. The sounds of scruffy neighborhood kids playing tag and stickball in the narrow street carried through our living room windows. Their moms and dads nursed icy cans of Schmidt's on their front stoops.

When I looked at the wedding photos, I didn't see exactly what I wanted to see. What I wanted to see was my dream wedding. I wanted to see myself costumed in that cream-colored jersey gown and hooded cape. I wanted to see myself in Mark's arms gliding across a checkered-tile dance floor like an Elizabethan courtesan. I wanted to see my two sisters and sister-in-law in their coral versions of my dress doing the same with their own chosen partners. I hadn't taken into account that the dance floor in the basement of Sisterhood Hall in the synagogue where we were married would be an institutional tan-and-gray linoleum installed after the Susquehanna River floodwaters of Hurricane Agnes ruined the basement of every house and structure along the riverfront. Drama aside, I'd expected to see the bride's and groom's gleaming smiles and the joyous expressions on the faces of the one hundred guests that we so carefully selected to keep the wedding small. In photo after photo, Mark and I stood as frozen as the tiny plastic bride and groom topping the three-tiered wedding cake. The only thing that changed in the pictures were those surrounding us. In the separate pictures of the families, each mother stood with grim, gritted teeth. Each father with the requisite smile of "Cheese."

When I thought about those photos as I sat alone in that hotel room, there was one in particular that troubled me. It was the iconic picture of the bride and her father entering the sanctuary. In the picture, my father in his chocolate-brown rented tuxedo and matching kippah looked joyous. I looked anything but happy. In fact, I looked outright glum. I wasn't prepared for that moment of our entrance. I was surprised to see all the guests stand up and turn to look at me. No one had told me about that tradition. My emotions read on my face as terror. My eyes were teary. It was as if I'd somehow ended up in the wrong place at the wrong time. In a movie I wasn't supposed to star in.

In all the wedding albums and bridal magazines I had seen until then, the brides had broad, toothy smiles. Their bright eyes sparkled with anticipation, not fear. Mine looked like a deer's in the headlights, and if there'd been a cartoon bubble above my head, it would have said: "Get me out of here! Will someone, anyone, please get me out of here?"

The romance between Mark and me had been short. On our six-week anniversary of dating, Mark cautiously took a small blue velvet box from the inside breast pocket of his tweed sports jacket and offered it across a candlelit table at The Arches, one of Philadelphia's iconic Greek Restaurants. I'd already been invited to dinner with his parents in their renovated Victorian in Society Hill. But I had not seen this moment coming. I don't recall ever discussing the possibility of marriage. I honestly don't.

The waiter, a young man dressed in standard black pants and a starched white open-collared shirt, who had just returned to the table with a basket of bread and butter, bore witness to all of this. I'm going to guess that what he saw on my face was an expression of shock. Maybe a half smile. Maybe confusion in a knitted brow. That was all on the outside. On the inside, adrenaline was surging through every cell of my body.

I don't know how long it took for my brain to place myself in the scene I was appearing in. To understand that Mark was proposing marriage. I can only say that I was grateful he didn't rise from the table and go down on one knee. In that moment, I wanted some perfect sign that I was truly in love with him. That he was my soul mate. That he was the man I wanted to live the rest of my life with, to have children with.

For reasons I can't explain now, I did what so many generations of women had done before me. Generations of women who weren't brave enough to say no, thank you, because we were conditioned to say yes. Pairing with another for life was what was expected. Like me, Mark was Jewish. He was from a good family, a mensch, my mother said. Perhaps this was the way it was supposed to be. I processed all this in less than thirty seconds. Then I reached across the table for that blue velvet box and prepared to say yes. Then I did. I said, "Yes."

Mark, who seemed to have stopped breathing in the freeze-frame of that moment, started breathing again. He smiled and slipped a perfectly sized diamond ring onto my right ring finger.

Years later, when Jerry and I were dining on a Seine River cruise in Paris, I saw those same mixed emotions on the face of a young woman two tables away from us as her date kneeled at her side and proffered a similarly small velvet box. The young woman looked confused, almost frightened. The memory of Mark's proposal flooded over me, and my heart raced right alongside hers. I don't know what choice that twenty-first century young woman made. But given the shocked expression on her face, I'd like to think she took more time than I did to reply. I want to think she is happy with whatever choice she made.

Looking back, I can see that my lack of conviction may have been an omen of things to come for us. Things hadn't gone well with the wedding plans. Mark's parents and mine were locked in a power struggle over the use of his family chuppah, the canopy that shelters Jewish couples during the marriage ceremony. There was a long line of Mark's family married under that chuppah. Mark's Grandpa Jack had brought it with him from the old country in Russia when he emigrated to the United States. Apparently, until our wedding, no one in his family had run into someone as contentious and opinionated as my mother. She wanted no part of that plush burgundy velvet covering with the thick twisted gold fringe. Our synagogue had a perfectly suitable chuppah, thank you very much, she said.

In the end, Mark's family won out and the heirloom chuppah was held up at the four corners with bamboo poles by Mark's three best men and his dad. Mark stamped on the ceremonial glass and, in the eyes of God, our marriage was sealed.

The whole affair had forced Mark and me to take sides in a way that was very difficult for such a young couple whose romantic love was already starting to fade. Within three months, Mark's parents weren't talking to either of us, and my parents were at best cool to the man I married.

"All men's miseries," wrote seventeenth-century philosopher Blaise Pascal, "derive from not being able to sit in a quiet room alone." Try wrapping your head around that one the next time you're alone.

VI
Letters

I would imagine there was a certain amount of restlessness among all of us held in this peculiar form of captivity, particularly when days passed without another juror being added. The court officers were getting less attentive. The taste of the restaurant food was getting stale and a handful of jurors were grousing at the prohibition of ordering steak and lobster from the dinner menu. Complaints to the court officers fell on deaf ears. "Send your complaints to the judge," they told us. Several of the jurors did just that. I suspected the judge had listened when at dinner one evening a cheer rose from the dining room table and high fives were exchanged among the steak-and-lobster lobbyists. The officers had just told them that steak and lobster were in. It was a very small victory.

I wasn't particularly interested in steak or lobster. I ate the simpler things on the menu. The foods I enjoyed at home. Lightly scrambled eggs without bacon, or a grilled medium-rare hamburger when the kitchen could get it right. Sometimes a warm cup of soup would get me through the day. No fish or seafood. From looking at the plates of others I could tell it wasn't fresh. And absolutely no reheated baked potatoes. When it came to the food, if I could have changed anything, it would have been the persistent preset chunk of iceberg lettuce smothered in lumpy orange dressing.

But that's not really where my gripe was. It seemed to me that being sequestered with no end in sight was cruel and unusual punishment. If I remembered correctly from my high school civics class, that should have been prohibited by the Eighth Amendment to the United States Constitution. It all boiled down to a violation of my constitutional rights. I spent a considerable amount of time scheming on a way to get a lawyer to take my case, but with no mail or connection to the outside world, I abandoned the idea.

In the moments when thoughts of my civil rights slid to the back burner, it was juror #3, Cheryl Ann Russo, that I locked my attention on. While it was true that most of the jurors would have preferred to be somewhere else, no one with the exception of Cheryl Ann Russo was crying and begging to go home. I'm not a medical professional, but it seemed to me that her level of distraction was very close to the line of obsession manifested by some kind of psychological illness.

On the night of the twelfth day of sequestration, I asked one of the court officers for a sheet of blank paper and a pen and wrote my own letter to the judge. I was careful to show respect, but I laid it out this way: *Locking up people with strangers for an unknown period of time is not likely to render justice. I can't speak for everyone here, but I believe that most of us would prefer to go home.* I'd give anything if I could see that letter today.

When I wrote that letter, it was one of the few times I thought about Freddy Burton in prison. By my calculation, he'd been locked up for at least three years—more than a thousand days, 24,000 hours—from the time of the wardens' murders to the time of this trial. I had to ask myself exactly what I was whining about. I was beginning to wonder if sequestering our jury was a ploy by the defense attorney to gain empathy for his client. To instill in jurors an idea of the lengths someone would go to if their rights had been unfairly taken away.

Christ, I thought I knew exactly how it would feel. I was willing to rappel down fourteen floors on the exterior of a Center City hotel. And I was no longer sure that there was no circumstance in which I would kill another human being.

But the gist of my letter to the judge was about Cheryl Ann Russo. About how unfit she was to serve. I wasn't the only one who doubted this sad woman's ability to render a fair verdict. Even Willard, who kept to himself for the most part, seemed to come apart at the seams when Cheryl Ann tearfully repeated her recipe for homemade spaghetti sauce. We all missed our lives. Our husbands. Our pets. Even our jobs. For Cheryl Ann, it was her red sauce. And it seemed nearly impossible for her to focus on anything else. Looking back on it, that sauce that she so lovingly—religiously—prepared for her husband must have been what made Cheryl Ann's life bearable. Without it, she didn't exist. Her constant recitations were driving more than one of us to the brink of insanity.

You should know, Your Honor, I wrote, *that Cheryl Ann Russo doesn't belong here. For the sake of her own sanity, the sanity of the entire jury, and in the interest of justice, Mrs. Russo should be dismissed and sent home.*

If someone got steak and lobster, I thought, maybe Cheryl Ann could get some relief and so could everyone else.

I carefully folded my letter in thirds and walked down the hall to the court officers' room. The door was open. Two uniformed officers were kicking back on the bed playing cards. In the background, Smokey Robinson was crooning from a small transistor radio on the nightstand. I stood in the doorway for a minute, not wanting to interrupt. One of the officers (I chose to never know their names) looked up and just stared at me. If words were put to that look they would have said, "What the hell do you want?"

"I'd like to have this letter taken to the judge. Can you do that?"

"Sure," said the officer as she shuffled the deck for the third time. "We can do that." I handed over the letter, and the officer set it down on the bed next to her. I had the uncomfortable feeling that my letter might never actually reach the judge and that maybe the steak-and-lobster win was the doing of the hotel staff and not the judge at all.

VII
Mother, Jugs & Speed

I will never know how or why it happened, but midday one day we were instructed to line up again at the elevator. In very short order we'd become good little chickens and did what we were told. It seemed things would turn out better that way. When we reached the lobby, at the officer's command, we lined up in pairs and were escorted out of the building. Those in the front of the line were the first to know where we were going. As quick as a game of Telephone, those of us in the back of the line knew we were marching a short distance to a nearby movie theater. The care that was being taken with us seemed extraordinary. I couldn't help but wonder if out there on the street we were in some kind of danger.

Once inside the theater, an usher escorted our entourage to a staircase at the left of the refreshment stand that was stocked with small, medium, and bucket-sized bags of buttered popcorn and oversize boxes of Good & Plenty and Junior Mints. Strung across the bottom of the staircase was a dark red velvet-covered rope. The usher ceremoniously lifted the brass hook from the stanchion and led us up the staircase to the theater's balcony. It seemed this wasn't the first time the theater had hosted a group like ours. We took our seats in an orderly fashion and waited. It was a weekday afternoon and the large art deco theater below us was nearly empty. There we were. Eight strangers, isolated under guard in a theater balcony in the middle of the afternoon waiting to watch the one-star-rated *Mother, Jugs & Speed*. The film starred Raquel Welch, Bill Cosby, and Harvey Keitel as ambulance drivers. It was certainly not a movie I would have chosen, and I wondered which of my fellow jurors agreed. And why the balcony?

"I know why we're up here," whispered Alene. "I'll tell you later." I'm not sure why, but throughout my sequestration I had a sense that talking at length with the other jurors was frowned on. Too great a risk that we'd complain to each other or talk about what one or the other of us knew about the case we were about to hear. Though I knew nothing about it and had nothing important to share, I was always more than curious about what Alene knew.

I remember little of that movie outing, other than the forced march to the theater, the obscure seating in the balcony, and thinking that the well-endowed Welch was an unlikely ambulance driver.

"This is Burton's second trial for the prison murders," Alene confided to me as we stepped outside the theater after the film. "The first ended in a mistrial when the jury witnessed a purse snatching in the hotel lobby."

Ah, that explained the degree of security. This was the second go-round, and the court officers had learned the hard way from their mistakes. Likely under the judge's orders, they were to be overly cautious with this set of jurors. And they were.

I chose the seat next to Alene at dinner that night. As I passed the basket of Parker House rolls and butter, I looked to my left toward the court officers before I spoke. The officers were busy chatting. The coast was clear.

"Do you know why he was in jail in the first place?" I whispered to her, never taking my eyes off the bread basket. Just as I had done before speaking to her, Alene looked first to her left and then her right. Then she simply nodded yes and said nothing more.

VIII
The Judge

What I know about the Honorable Lawrence Prattis I know from his obituary. Judge Prattis (1927–2003) was one of several African American judges on the Common Pleas Court of Philadelphia bench at the time of the Burton trial. The Philadelphia Bar Association's "Legends of the Bar" recognized him for outstanding jurisprudence and his dedication to the city's low-income housing. Though he handled mostly civil cases, it may have been his calm demeanor and courtroom-management skills that earned him the abiding respect of the city's trial lawyers. For those skills, he was no doubt a good choice to preside over the Burton trial, where the potential for chaos loomed.

The crime had raised the hackles of Philadelphia's mayor, Frank Rizzo, who didn't miss the opportunity to wave the banner for the death penalty in cases like this. This trial would have to be run like a tight ship, and Judge Prattis was the man for the job.

From the judge's obituary, I know he spent his leisure time tending roses, listening to all kinds of music, and deep-sea fishing off the shores of Cape May, New Jersey, where he and his family had a vacation home.

On Memorial Day weekend in 1976, when the jury sequestered

for the Burton trial was grounded in a downtown hotel, I imagine Judge Prattis on his boat off the Jersey coast at Cape May, casting for the ocean's fish du jour. On his desk in city hall may have been a stack of handwritten letters from members of the jury. The first among the jurors had been sequestered for almost two weeks, and the jury's impatience was reaching a breaking point. Letters from more than one juror reported that juror #3's incessant pleading to go home to prepare homemade spaghetti sauce for her husband of twenty-five years was more than they could bear. In twenty-five years, apparently her husband had never been left on his own to prepare a meal.

It seemed a bit too much panic over a frantic Italian woman going off-kilter about pasta sauce. The right jurors for this case were hard to come by. Juror #3, he thought, wasn't going anywhere.

An honest judge like Judge Prattis wasn't likely to quarrel with their complaints. He too may have been frustrated with the glacial pace of jury selection, the petty quarreling between the two attorneys, and maybe even the pressure from higher-ups for a guilty verdict and the reinstitution of the death penalty.

But more important to the judge may have been his knowledge that a frustrated jury wasn't likely to render a fair verdict, particularly when the only thing on their minds was going home. The long holiday weekend meant they wouldn't start their real service for another three days. Though the movie outing had done little to calm the ferment brewing among the jurors, Judge Prattis ordered another outing on this holiday weekend, when the smell of barbecue simmered in the jurors' backyards without them. Something with a bit more glamour than *Mother, Jugs & Speed*. Something more upscale. He instructed the court officers to take the disgruntled bunch on a one-day field trip to New Hope, a lovely tourist mecca on the Delaware River forty miles north of Philadelphia. Maybe that would show how much their service was appreciated. The only thing I remember about that trip is the bus ride and the way the court officer cleared the public restroom of others when I needed to use the bathroom.

As I piece together this story, I wonder if the slow pace of the jury selection was only a part of what weighed heavily on the judge's mind. Maybe it was the defendant, Frederick Burton, and what may have been a wrongful conviction for the murder charges that landed him in prison in the first place. In the years since his conviction, more than one petition had been filed on Burton's behalf, raising the matter of an allegedly coerced testimony by the key witness against him as well as some alleged carefully orchestrated maneuvers by the DA's office that had kept an immunity document from him and his attorney.

Burton was twenty-five years old when he was arrested for the murder of Officer Von Colln. He had been on his way to living the American dream. He'd attended John Bartram High School in Southwest Philadelphia and had played on the school's basketball team. He had a steady job with Bell Telephone. He was a family man with a young son and daughter and twins on the way. And though racial conflict openly festered in many Philadelphia neighborhoods, Burton had somehow managed to steer clear of the raging violence between the police and members of the African American community. Before his arrest in the Von Colln murder, Frederick Burton had not had a single run-in with the law. The pieces didn't fit.

Like Freddy, Judge Prattis was a lifelong resident of Philadelphia. He graduated from West Philadelphia High School, then college at Howard University and law school at Temple University, where he was editor of *Temple Law Review*. I wonder if he was ever treated with anything but respect. If he or anyone in his family ever had an unpleasant encounter with law enforcement of any kind. He had sons and a grandson. What about them? Had this African American judge been privileged in some way that Freddy was not?

Somehow I know Judge Prattis was a good man. A man that may have felt Freddy Burton's pain, even if there was nothing he could do about it. So, as I imagine him hauling in the day's catch in a bucket of ice up the dock toward his summer home, I think he may have known there was little hope that Burton would be—could be—acquitted. Captain of the Guards Leroy Taylor was in the warden's office that day. He saw Burton thrusting something into Bob Fromhold's bloodstained back. Fromhold was dead, Taylor himself injured, and Burton strangely silent. These grisly murders happened, and it should have been simple. But it simply wasn't.

The judge must have understood that prison did things to people. Holmesburg was inhumanely overcrowded. The inmates were dangerous. Many of the guards were callous and cautious. Status was king, among the guards and prisoners and among the prisoners themselves. Good souls didn't last long in prison.

The honorable judge's consolation? The law. I believe it was his bible, a safe space inside which he could operate. The law must trump the heart, he likely thought. The law had a way of making things right. Burton's trial would be fair. The judge would see to that. And perhaps one day, his earlier conviction might be revisited. It was time for something to go in this young man's favor. A young man who may have been in the wrong place at the wrong time, twice.

IX
The Terrordome

No single experience in my life could have prepared me to understand life inside Holmesburg Prison or how it might come to pass that two Black inmates could be involved in the murders of two white wardens. Even today, that situation seems implausible. But it did happen. And it may be that it happened at Holmesburg because at the time, Holmesburg surpassed many other correctional institutions on the scale of violence and the dehumanization its prisoners experienced. For the people incarcerated there, it's unlikely that a single day in the hundred-year history of this institution was free of some form of intimidation—inmates against inmates, inmates against guards, or guards against inmates.

Freddy Burton was transferred from Eastern State Penitentiary to Holmesburg in 1971 and was imprisoned there until the wardens were slain in 1973. He spent much of that time in solitary confinement. I can't know what brutality Mr. Burton may have suffered in those years, but Holmesburg's history is replete with insidious acts of cruelty against the inmates imprisoned there. This story would not be complete without an account of some of the most horrific incidents that took place in what was known as the "Terrordome."

On August 20, 1938, twenty-five prisoners who led a prison-wide hunger strike were locked for a weekend in the Klondike "bake-oven." The Klondike was a small concrete isolation block lined with radiators and steam pipes. Punishment consisted of locking prisoners inside with no food or water, turning up the heat, locking the windows and air vents, and raising the inside temperature to unbearable heights. That August, with an oppressive heatwave recording daily temperatures near one hundred degrees, the temperature inside the Klondike rose to a deadly two hundred degrees, only twelve degrees below boiling. For three days, prison officials ignored the desperate cries for help from inside the block. When guards finally opened the door, four men were dead and many others nearly so. According to doctors, the men were essentially "scalded to death."

Between 1951 and 1974, University of Pennsylvania dermatologist Dr. Albert M. Kligman performed a variety of barbarous medical experiments on thousands of Holmesburg inmates. His experiments exposed them to viruses, skin-blistering chemicals, radiation therapies, psychoactive drugs, and dioxins. Experiments that were funded by such sponsors as Johnson & Johnson, Dow Chemical, and the US Army. Prisoners were paid as little as ten dollars for their participation. It's been written that none were advised of risks or treated in timely ways for complications that arose. Some said that Holmesburg prisoners could be identified by their burn scars from experimental skin tests. In the most gruesome accounts, pieces of cadavers were stitched into the backs of inmates to determine if they could grow back into functioning organs.

In 1970, just two months before Freddy's arrest, nearly one hundred inmates armed with meat cleavers, boning knives, makeshift pitchforks, and table legs destroyed the dining hall and assaulted other inmates and guards. As many as one hundred were injured in what became known as the Independence Day Riot. Mayor Rizzo blamed African American prisoners, who he claimed attacked white inmates and guards. Prison-reform organizations countered that overcrowding and abuse by guards were what fanned the sparks that ignited the violence. Violence that had long been woven into the fabric of daily life in Holmesburg.

In 1973, the prison that was built to house seven hundred men was crammed with twelve hundred.

In 1995, the antiquated nineteenth-century structure was closed and decommissioned.

The absence of creature comforts in Holmesburg was a given. But I imagine the rarest commodity in the corridors and cellblocks of this antediluvian structure was trust. Inmates were segregated by race, and Muslim inmates were segregated by sects. Some 80 percent of the inmates were Black; most prison officials were white. The line between friendship and enmity was all too often razor-thin. Some say that underneath it all was a culture of savage gang warfare between cellblocks that was carefully cultivated by the prison administration. No one was safe.

I imagine in the nearly two years there that Freddy awaited his trial for the Von Colln murder, his moods would have shifted from terror to resignation and then to empowerment. He would survive because he'd done nothing wrong. He would return to his family and be a present father to his children. He would hold hope for the time he could celebrate Christmas crowded around the family's dining room table. Hope to go back to his job splicing lines for Bell Telephone and bringing home a paycheck. Hope to once again shoot one-on-one hoops at the corner park. Hope for everything freedom would offer him.

His true sustenance, though, may have come from the brotherhood he found among fellow inmates at weekly Muslim prayer meetings in the prison's community room. By 1972, on the eve of his trial for the Von Colln murder, he'd exchanged his slave name, or given name, Freddy, for the Muslim name Muhammed. And on the day of his trial, he arrived at the courthouse in a classic Black Islam robe with a white scarf draped over his head.

On his best days, I envision Freddy did all he could to preserve his faith in what he knew to be true. He was not guilty of Officer Von Colln's murder.

X
The Trial

On the fifteenth day of our sequestration, after yet another breakfast of lumpy, lukewarm oatmeal in the hotel dining room, the other jurors and I were led back to our rooms one last time before the starting gun for the trial was to be fired.

For most of that last week, the details of my room no longer held interest for me. The room was a stage set in which I'd performed the same actions for so many days of a long run that the set designer's carefully chosen minutia was lost on me. The chink in the wall behind the door where a doorstop should have been, the brown stain at the corner of the rug, those 486 white ceramic tiles, and the lone splat of bird crap on the window had all just become parts of a whole. Though I did still occasionally wonder if and when someone in a harness and hard hat on a scaffold would ascend the side of the building with an oversized squeegee to wipe away the offending spatter.

Teeth brushed, hair combed, and errant eyebrow hairs plucked, I opened the door to the hallway, closed it behind me, and headed to the elevator, where the first shift of jurors had already departed for the ground-floor lobby. No one spoke on the elevator ride. Once in the lobby, like shushed school children we waited for the elevator to deliver the last jurors from the hotel's fourteenth floor. Then, as we'd been trained, we fell in line in pairs to leave the building. I still paired with Alene. With Alene, I felt safe.

"Well, this is it," she whispered as we exited the hotel onto Walnut Street.

"Yeah, this will be over soon."

We walked in pairs the two blocks to city hall. I kept my eyes on the pavement, stepping over the lines and cracks in a game I often played as a child: *Step on a crack, break your mother's back. Step on a line, break your mother's spine.*

Alene walked with her head held high. I wondered if she'd ever played the sidewalk game. What was also worthy of note that morning was that Alene looked as if she'd dressed for church. She wore a lovely floral dress, hemmed just below the knee, and an orchid-colored silk scarf wrapped around her neck. Her smooth coffee-with-cream-colored skin was the perfect complement to her outfit.

By then, Mark must have created a routine with the court officers to bring me clean clothes each week. I don't remember what I was wearing that first day of the trial, but I do remember having a penchant for simple black slacks and a favorite black-and-white pin-striped Oxford-style shirt that I still have hanging in my closet. It's an outfit I would still choose today.

Without warning, Alene reached over, took my hand, and squeezed it tight. "I know you're scared, but this is going to be OK. We're near the end. That Black boy doesn't have a chance."

I looked into her eyes, and she gently looked back into mine. No more words were spoken.

The twelve of us filed into city hall's Room 253 from a side entrance and took our seats in the jury box in the order of our selection. Juror #4's seat, my seat, looked as if it was the best seat in the house. Front row, stage left. Closest to the witness stand. So close, I only had to lean over the low wall in front of the jury box to touch it. Freddy Burton and his lawyer were already seated at the defense table. The only sound was the shuffling of the last spectators taking their seats in the gallery's polished wooden chairs. Among the spectators, I noticed several Black men wearing colorful Muslim prayer caps.

The baritone voice of a white gentlemanly court officer broke the silence. "Oyez! Oyez! Oyez! All rise for the Honorable Lawrence Prattis. The hearing in the case of the State of Pennsylvania against Frederick Burton is about to begin."

I stood for the judge, as did all the others in the room. I didn't know then that the origin of the court officer's cry was from the French word *ouïr*, meaning "to hear." I didn't know that "Oyez, oyez" was first used by the Anglo-Normans, the white medieval ruling class in England.

I confess to never meeting Freddy Burton in person. What I know about who he was and is, I've learned from others. When I reflect on the experience of the trial though, I imagine what it must have been like for Freddy on that day. The day he was shuttled from his cell in solitary and transferred in a prison van to the courtroom inside city hall. That day may have been the first time he'd felt a moment of warm sun in thirty-six months. In the "hole," there were no seasons. There was no sun or moon or wind or rain. There were no stars. There was only time. Time under the twenty-four-hour glare of humming fluorescent tubes and the smell of dense sweat from a thousand men. Freddy Burton had not been tenderly touched by another human being in more than a thousand days.

Those who knew him knew a strong-willed, generous man. A man who, when cloistered in a cell no larger than a horse stall, could remain whole, unbroken. He might have passed the hours pacing and praying and reading. They could take away his freedom, he thought. But they could not take away his soul. That was his and his alone. Swallowed up in that cell, I imagine he could have learned every verse of the Koran by heart.

While others have disintegrated after three years in solitary confinement, that day in the courtroom Freddy Burton could only be described as grounded. He sat upright in his chair. His eyes closed. His head bowed as if in prayer. I can't know what his silent affect meant, but on that day, seated at the defense table, his inner strength was palpable. To some, his appearance may have been simply humble. To others, it may have spoken of pride. To others still, it shouted unflagging defiance.

Prosecuting attorney Bill Knauer was one of the district attorney's wunderkinder. But at thirty-four years old, the fair-skinned man of slight stature and thinning blond hair appeared to be no match for the grandiose style of his courtroom opponent, Cecil Bassett Moore.

Moore was a Marine Corps veteran and a zealous civil rights activist who never backed down from a fight. He marched, he protested, and he spoke out sharply against the lack of Black representation in labor unions, against segregated schools, and against racial bias in the workforce.

It was Moore's no-holds-barred personal style that earned him both friends and enemies in Philadelphia's roiling political climate. He was known to represent the underrepresented. Frederick Burton's case suited Cecil Moore like the best-fitting pair of gloves.

Of course, I knew none of this at the time and could only judge Mr. Moore by what I saw and heard. His shimmery three-piece suit, his highly polished leather shoes, and his gruff manner all translated to unseemly showmanship that bordered on a lack of respect for courtroom decorum. If asked at the time, I would have favored Bill Knauer's less combative prep-school style. Years later I would wonder if what really made Knauer seem more credible to me was that he was white.

Knauer was anything but a grandstander. Instead, it was his unwavering dedication to a conviction that gave him a very strong hand. In his opening argument, he described the bloodbath that took place in the warden's office: Warden Patrick Curran, stabbed six times, dead; his deputy Bob Fromhold, stabbed thirteen times, dead. Captain of the Guards Leroy Taylor, wounded. Knauer balanced the grim detail of the crimes with a calm and even delivery that communicated authority and truth.

"You will hear testimony from the only surviving witness, Captain Leroy Taylor, and there will be no reasonable doubt in your minds that on May 31, 1973, Mr. Burton and Mr. Bowen entered Deputy Fromhold's office with the intention to assassinate the warden with hand-hewn mess hall knives."

Knauer walked us through his version of the day the murders took place. His slow-paced account of the violence was almost surreal. A nightmare that begs waking up from. I found myself looking away from him and over his right shoulder to other faces in the courtroom. And I distracted myself by focusing on the expressionless face of the defendant. In spite of the vile accusations being made about him, Freddy Burton barely lifted his gaze from his clasped hands on the table in front of him. I have a memory of Moore tipping back in his chair and steadying himself on the chair's two back legs. I am certain that in his teeth was a stubby half-smoked cigar.

Three seats to my right, Cheryl Ann was wringing a shredded tissue in her plump fingers. One seat past Cheryl, Alene was looking directly into her own horizon, still holding her well-kept secret about the defendant and how all this came to pass. Willard, as always, appeared unaffected. The eyes of the spectators were glued to the jury box.

In his opening argument, Moore wasted no time setting up for the jury the grim, violent, and hopeless lives of prisoners behind Holmesburg's stone walls—deadly rival gangs and inhumane solitary confinement, all in violation of anyone's civil rights.

"On May 31, 1973, Mr. Burton and his fellow inmate Joseph Bowen were called to the warden's office to discuss their request for more time in the prison's community room for daily prayer services. Searched twice by the guards, the two men were unarmed when they were admitted to the office. I intend to prove," Moore continued, "that Deputy Warden Fromhold himself took the murder weapons from his desk drawer, where he kept contraband items from prison inmates. I intend to prove that Deputy Warden Fromhold threatened to plant those knives in the inmates' cells. Then, he informed Mr. Burton and Mr. Bowen that when the weapons were found in routine cell searches, the two inmates would be transferred to the cellblock of a rival Muslim faction." Such a transfer, Moore contended, was tantamount to a threat of serious violence if not murder. "You will hear from Mr. Burton's codefendant Joseph Bowen that when the melee in the warden's office took place, Mr. Burton froze. That Mr. Burton called out to Mr. Bowen to 'Cool it.' That Mr. Burton did not participate at all in the murders."

When Knauer called Captain Taylor to the witness stand, only the last of the court recorder's muted keystrokes could be heard. Captain of the Guards Leroy Taylor had been seriously wounded when he attempted to stop the confrontation in the warden's office. He was the prosecution's key witness against Mr. Burton. A middle-aged, dignified Black man in suit and tie, Captain Taylor spoke easily as he told the jury that when he entered the warden's office, he saw Deputy Warden Fromhold curled in a fetal position on the floor and Freddy thrusting his hand in a stabbing motion into Fromhold's blood-soaked shirt. As the captain spoke the words, he raised his fist and thrust it toward his lap several times. Just as he described what he saw.

I don't recall ever seeing the shivs in a marked-as-an-exhibit plastic evidence bag or even if the bag was passed around the jury box as I've seen on television dramas. But I wouldn't be surprised if Knauer was holding up such a bag as he paced back and forth in the narrow pathway where the witness stand and jury box intersected.

Though my senses had been dulled after two weeks of sequestration, now they were on high alert, and I recall considering that my "best seat in the house" in the jury box may not have been a blessing after all. It was only the soothing effect of Judge Prattis that settled my nerves. Maybe it was the authority vested in him by his black robe, or the upright, confident way he sat in his chair, or the way he seemed to pay attention to every detail before him without judgment. What Judge Prattis afforded in the courtroom was a sense of order and competence. Both in stark contrast to the story unfolding before me.

For the umpteenth time since this chapter of my life began, my mind was wandering. How did the district attorney's day unfold before going to court that morning? Was he the sort to look in the mirror at his nearly colorless eyes and give himself a pep talk or practice his opening argument? What did he have for breakfast? Was he as frustrated with the delays in jury selection as I was? How confident was he that he would win this case? I imagined he had two children, two years apart, that he dropped off at Germantown Friends School in the morning. I was curious about what he read while seated in a leather recliner in his den lined with shelves stocked with books on American history. And I asked myself how someone so young could land a case like this. Knauer's voice pulled me back to the proceedings: "I have no more questions for this witness, Your Honor."

As Knauer took his seat, Moore clopped his tilted chair to the floor, stood up, and rested a hand of assurance on Freddy's shoulder. Then he balanced his unlit cigar on the railing that separated the defense table from the spectators and stalked up to Captain Taylor on the witness stand.

"Did you see a knife in Mistuh Burton's hand?" he asked, his Southern drawl punctuating the words *Did* and *knife*. Captain Taylor shifted in the chair, leaned just a bit forward, and prepared to answer the question. In the few seconds it took the captain to find his words, Mr. Moore picked up his pace. "Yaas or no, Cap'n Taylor? Did you see a knife? Yaas or no! You say you saw him thrusting his hand into the warden's body. Did you see a knife? Anything silver or shiny in his hand that looked like a knife? Yaas or no, Cap'n Taylor?"

The captain's thick dark mustache flexed up and down. Across his forehead was the beginning of a line of perspiration. "I don't recall," he replied. Then the captain took his time once again thrusting his hand up and down, as if he were recalling what he'd seen, more slowly this time. "He was doing this."

"You *don't* recall if you saw a knife, Cap'n Taylor?" Moore barked.

Then, with the prowess of a basso profundo preacher from the pulpit, emphasizing each syllable of each word, Moore asked, "Is it possible, Cap'n Taylor, that in the rush of the moment, in the horror of what you saw, no single one of your recollections are representative of what really happened in the warden's office that day?"

"Objection, your honor," Knauer charged, jumping to his feet.

Moore glanced sideways at the jury box, wheeled around, and

walked back to the defense table. "Withdrawn, your honor. I have no more questions for this witness." Then Moore reached for his soggy stogie, clamped it between his teeth, and took his seat next to his client.

In March of 1975, Joseph "Joe-Joe" Bowen was convicted of two counts of first-degree murder for his part in the slaying of the Holmesburg wardens. On the day of his conviction, newspaper headlines that I read years later gave a clue to Joe-Joe's state of mind: "Wardens' Killer Grins at Guilt."

On this Saturday morning, when the hubbub of Philadelphia's street traffic had settled into its weekend calm, Bowen was transferred in an armed Department of Corrections van down Broad Street from Graterford Penitentiary to Judge Prattis's city hall courtroom. I remember seeing him in handcuffs. I can't be sure the cuffs weren't belly chained to a belt around his waist. Or if his ankles were also restrained. In my world, those extreme measures would have made sense for a convicted murderer. Maybe it was because he swaggered up to the witness stand with an awkward gate. I did feel frightened though. Frightened because my seat at the front corner of the jury box nearest the witness stand was closer than I wanted to be to this man.

When Bowen took his seat in the witness stand, he slouched into the chair and planted his two feet on the stand's front railing. His unbuttoned sports jacket must have been prison issued. It looked just like the one Freddy was wearing. I wondered if there was a closet full of them at the prison where inmates with court dates were costumed before their appearances. Unlike Freddy though, Joe-Joe wore a pair of black-plastic-framed eyeglasses that reminded me of the ones I'd seen in photos of Malcolm X.

Also unlike Freddy, there was nothing withdrawn about Joe-Joe.

His right eye seemed to float up toward the bridge of his nose. His left zoomed scornfully across the jury box and the observers in the courtroom. For reasons I don't recall, Bowen was questioned by his own attorney.

"Mr. Bowen, please tell the jury where you reside."

Joe-Joe looked down toward his feet on the railing and spoke only three words: "In the hole."

"Mr. Bowen, once again, please tell the jury where you reside."

Three words: "In the hole."

"For the record," translated the attorney, "the hole is solitary confinement at Graterford Penitentiary. Mr. Bowen, can you tell us what happened on May 31, 1973, in the deputy warden's office at Holmesburg?"

Joe-Joe responded with a look I can only describe as arrogant.

"Mr. Bowen, you are here to testify on behalf of Frederick Burton, seated at the defense table. It would be in his best interest if you would tell the jury what happened that day in the deputy warden's office."

Bowen was still precariously leaning back in the same witness chair I sat in just weeks before at the *voir dire*. His shackled wrists rested in his lap, and the line of his lips was in a half smile. It was chilling to be in his presence. I thought at the time that was the way he wanted it.

"I killed the pigs!"

"Was Frederick Burton in the deputy warden's office with you that day?"

"Yeah—but I killed those pigs. Freddy was there. But Freddy didn't do anything. He just stood there petrified. He kept telling me to cool it."

If it had been a movie, the director would have told Bowen to raise a clenched, shackled wrist above his head and hold it there. End scene.

Bowen's testimony was so shocking to me that I have no memory of Moore or Knauer cross-examining him. But it didn't matter.

There you have it. That's it. All I knew. In the six days of the trial, Freddy Burton never took the stand, raised his right hand, and swore to tell the truth, his truth of what happened in the deputy warden's office. For me, it all boiled down to one of two choices. I could believe a prison official with a questionable recollection of witnessing two grisly murders in the making, or I could believe a seemingly deranged, self-proclaimed convicted killer. The only place those two narratives crossed over were the facts that the wardens were dead and Joe-Joe and Freddy were in the room when it happened.

There is one more thing—probably the most important thing I can tell you about the logic at the time of my choice to convict Freddy Burton: the judge's instructions to the jury. To the best of my recollection, the judge carefully instructed us regarding the law. If Mr. Burton was present in the warden's office when the murders took place, he told us, then he should be found guilty. You may not like that law, he said, but that is the law. I know this sounds implausible if not outright wrong. Maybe that's why his words registered so deeply with me. Or maybe it was because it made the decision about Freddy Burton's guilt or innocence so clear. If he was in the room, he was guilty. After all, what were we being asked to do? We were being asked to decide if Freddy Burton broke the law. Looking back all these years later, I can still feel the beginning of relief coming over me.

This is almost over. It's a slam dunk. He was in the room. He's guilty. I can go home now. For the first time, Cheryl Ann and I were on the same page. I could smell and taste my own simple cooking. I could feel the warmth of my husband's body cuddled next to me at night. I could call my sister and weep with relief. I could go back to work. I could put these miserable twenty-one days behind me.

I have to tell you that I've searched the Internet for any legal reference to what I thought I heard Judge Prattis say so many years ago. I can't find one, and the transcript of the trial no longer exists in the box that's been archived among those city hall records from nearly fifty years ago.

I can tell you now without reservation that if I knew then what I know now—if I was the person I am today rather than the person I was then—I would have found Freddy Burton not guilty. Even if I was the lone holdout and hung the jury. And I would have walked away knowing I did the right thing for Freddy Burton.

But I was who I was on that coolish day in June when our jury was marched off to deliberate. And this is the sum total of what that twenty-four-year-old me knew and believed. I knew what Captain Taylor told us. I knew that he saw or thought he saw Freddy stabbing Warden Fromhold with a knife. I knew what Joe-Joe Bowen told us. That Freddy froze, petrified. That he shouted to Joe-Joe to cool it. I knew that according to the law, if Freddy was in the room, he was guilty. And I knew that all those things could not be true at the same time.

Willard was quickly established as the jury foreman. A good choice. Everyone liked him. He'd earned their respect. Out of the gate, we took a vote. I don't remember the tally of the first vote. I do remember it wasn't unanimous. And I remember being dumbfounded that, given the judge's instructions, anyone who heard what he said could vote not guilty. I was impatient. I took center stage and restated the judge's instructions. I remember thinking, *This guy, Freddy Burton? He's already in jail. Even if we acquit him, he isn't going home. Alene is right.*

"I'm not going to say I necessarily agree with the law. But the law is the law," I told them. I remember that bold assertion and the purposeful way I made my case. Dear God, couldn't they see that wrapping this up in the cleanest, most obvious way was our ticket home? The first real way out we had after so many days in sequestration? The law was the law.

I don't remember what the room we were in looked like. I don't remember hearing the ticking of a clock or if there even was one on the wall. I don't remember if there was a picture of Frank Rizzo watching over us or if they brought us food or dinner as the hours passed. I don't remember the arguments made or if the Black jurors or jurors older than me saw what was before them differently than I did. What I do remember of that day is in very slow motion, as if someone were cranking an old film projector by hand one faded frame at a time.

According to newspaper accounts at the time, it was three hours until we reached a unanimous verdict.

After we reentered the courtroom and took our seats, Willard delivered our verdict, and the judge instructed each of us to stand up alone and own it. To hear ourselves say the words out loud and to understand the gravity of each of our personal decisions to seal Freddy Burton's fate for life in a Pennsylvania prison. *Guilty of second-degree murder.* Those words spoken twelve times by twelve very different people for twelve very different reasons. *Guilty of second-degree murder.* As I stood to proclaim my own verdict, I could feel the perspiration soaking through my blouse. My fingertips were tingling from the pent-up energy of twenty-one days of sequestration. As I stood there, exposed, nothing felt safe.

Freddy Burton was on his feet behind the defense table, his six-foot frame hunched owl-like at his shoulders. I have to wonder now what thoughts were going through his mind as twelve strangers spoke words that would change his life in ways he'd never imagined. Each declaration a single drumbeat echoing louder and louder until he wanted to jump out of his skin. Did his chest rise and fall each time the words were spoken? Did he glance stone-faced behind him at family members among the spectators or fix his eyes on each juror as they spoke? *Guilty of second-degree murder.* I don't know. Because when I spoke my own words, I looked away from Freddy Burton. My job was done. I was going home.

Walking back to the Holiday Inn, no longer invisibly chained and in step with eleven others, we entered the hotel as free men and women. There were no mournful goodbyes or exchanges of phone numbers or promises of gatherings at some future time. Only relief. As we stepped off the elevator on the fourteenth floor for the last time, Alene stepped up close enough to me to whisper in my ear.

"You want to know what he did to get himself in jail in the first place?"

I no longer cared. "Okay, sure, tell me."

"He killed a white park policeman. It happened in 1970. He and a handful of others were Black Panthers or something like that. And they shot the officer five times. The papers were full of it."

With Alene's words, any doubt I might have had at the time about my choice to convict Freddy Burton disappeared. It seemed Alene was right all along. Freddy Burton was never getting out of jail.

XI
Blank Slates

We start our existence in this world with a blank slate, and we don't stop becoming fully who we are until we take our last breath. Every minute from our first breath to our last, something inside us is cataloging small fragments of thoughts or ideas or opinions or judgments about the world we live in. These bits and pieces condition us to be as much like those that came before us as possible. Many of the bits come from our parents and their parents and their parents before them. Like family recipes and heirlooms and tall tales of family quarrels among distant relatives from the old country, they are encoded in us. Equally powerful are those that come from our schools, our churches, or our synagogues where we learn to have blind faith. Others come from films and plays and books and art and music. And still others from our spouses or our lovers and eventually from our children. Countless as the stars in the Milky Way, these bits and pieces of information are encrypted into our hearts and minds in ways we may never comprehend. Together they shape what we believe about others, how they live, and how we engage with them.

It would be foolish of me to think I could decipher or catalog all of my own bits and pieces. But I do have a sense that it is the linking up of those pieces that set me on a path of white privilege and colored my world in ways that brought me to judge Freddy Burton the way I did.

The first bits appeared in January of 1951, when my mother peed into a little cup in the doctor's office and learned that she was pregnant with her third child, me. That wasn't supposed to happen, she lamented to close family and friends. She was still nursing my nine-month-old sister, Sue. You couldn't get pregnant if you were nursing. Or so she thought. Sorry, Mom.

My mother had other plans for her life before marriage and raising three daughters arrived at her doorstep. She was a gifted musician with a rich coloratura soprano voice that earned her solo performances in Pittsburgh's Heinz Chapel Choir. Somewhere in the depths of family lore, I think there may have been a concert at Carnegie Hall too, or at least the option of one. Before she married my father in 1945, she'd sung at the weddings of more than three hundred others. In her twenties, she changed her given surname, Goldstein, to her stage name, Gould, to disguise her Jewish heritage. Music was her life. If her immigrant parents had permitted it, she would have accepted her admission to Juilliard School of Music in New York and attempted a career in opera. My mother practiced on the walnut baby grand piano in our living room nearly every day. Though many days she played and sang Italian love songs, most often it was *Kismet*'s "And This Is My Beloved."

By standards of the day, my mother was beautiful. She pampered herself from jars of Merle Norman cosmetics her entire life. Until she died at the age of eighty from a brain tumor, the skin on her face glowed like pearls—creamy, white, smooth, and unwrinkled. Until cancer made it too difficult to leave the house, she rarely missed her appointment at Lyman's salon on Third Street next to the Uptown movie theater, where he washed, occasionally colored, and styled her hair every Friday afternoon.

After I went off to college, my mother won a seat on the local city council. She raised money for the United Jewish Appeal and a local senior citizens' home and the city's first hospice residence. Anyone in the community who needed anything knew to call my mother. From her hospital bed in the hospice residence, I watched her call a local appliance dealer and wrangle a free refrigerator for the staff when the residence's refrigerator was on its last legs. Her name and civic contributions are inscribed on a plaque in front of Harrisburg's city hall. Her achievements and drive to see and be seen will always be a part of who I am.

She was mother to everyone except her three daughters, who could somehow never measure up to her expectations, just as she, I presume, could never live up to her own mother's expectations of her.

In spite of her outward success, my mother lived too many years of her life in a state of disappointment and regret. Regret for the loss of her musical career in exchange for marriage and family.

My mother gave birth to three children in four years. Too many by her standards. My oldest sister, Barbara, in 1948, Sue in 1950, and me in 1951. She did have domestic help with the three of us, mother's helpers who slept in a bedroom in the third-floor attic of our five-bedroom, two-and-a-half-bath duplex on the north side of town. Esther is the only mother's helper I recall. She left us when she married her boyfriend, Buck. We never saw her again. What was a joyous time for the newlyweds was my mother's worst nightmare because when Esther took her small suitcase of belongings from our attic bedroom, my mother was left on her own with the three of us.

My mother also employed cleaning ladies who twice a week did the laundry, dusted the tabletops, cleaned the bathrooms, and mopped and vacuumed the floors and carpets while she coffee-klatched with friends over small slices of Entenmann's coffee cake. Unlike Esther, who was white, our cleaning ladies were, in the vernacular of the day, colored. My mother referred to these adult women as her "girls." I knew them as Ezel and Anna and JoAnn. I never knew their last names.

My mother kept paper sacks of our outgrown dresses and coveralls and winter jackets that she generously offered to her "girls," though never without making the point of saying that otherwise they'd end up in a rummage sale somewhere. To my mother, giving these women first pick of our castoffs was an honorable thing to do, but it also saved her a trip to the thrift store to drop them off. Thinking back, if I had been Ezel or Anna or JoAnn, I'm not sure whether I would have seen this gesture as generous or demeaning.

Ezel, Anna, and JoAnn were the only African American people I knew. I treasured each of them for their willingness to connect with a family that was not their own, and I have wholehearted memories of the times they showed unconditional affection, if not love, toward me and my sisters.

When I was three and suffered my first bee sting, I pedaled my red tricycle as fast as I could home. Ezel was there, her arms ready to hug and her patience ready to ease my pain. I remember sitting on the lid of the green porcelain commode in our first-floor powder room gasping for air through my sobs. Ezel was kneeling in front of me, and the astringent smell of Bactine antiseptic flooded the air around us. Her words of comfort never stopped, and it remained a secret between the two of us from my mother that I was silly enough to study that bee on my finger until it stung me.

Anna, who wasn't much taller than Sue or I, endlessly joked

with us until we became proficient enough to tease her back. We loved spending time with her, and I have to believe she felt the same way about us. When my parents took their annual vacation to the Tanglewood Music Festival in Massachusetts, Anna babysat for us, making sure we were up and ready for summer camp in the mornings and had good meals for dinner at night.

When the curtain fell on my high school play and all the other kids' parents rushed backstage oozing pride over their progenies' performances, my own parents were absent. They were in the lobby seeing and being seen by the community at large. It was JoAnn, not my parents, who came to the green room. "You were wonderful," she said, handing me a bouquet of roses and squeezing me tight.

Ezel and Anna and JoAnn were there in so many ways that I preferred their genuinely caring attention to that of my parents.

Ezel was the darkest skinned of the three women. Then Anna. Then JoAnn. From time to time, out of their earshot, my mother spoke of them as her *schwarzes*, a derogatory Yiddish slur from the German word *schwarz*, meaning black. It makes me desperately sad that without knowing it, despite the loving care they lavished on me and my sisters, my mother's judgment of them as something less secretly found its way into the person I was becoming.

I grew up in a small, close-knit enclave of Jewish families in Pennsylvania's state capital of Harrisburg, just a hundred miles west on Interstate 76 from Philadelphia. My family home was a 1940s brick duplex in an upscale neighborhood one block from the Susquehanna River, which froze in the winter and came near flood stage every spring. Five hundred yards across the street was our family's synagogue, Temple Beth El. That's where my mother conducted the choir and my father served on the temple's board of directors. To make my world even smaller, my two sisters and I attended the city's only Hebrew day school, where the school day was evenly divided between Jewish instruction and whatever the state's school curriculum required. In this world, my sisters and I were spared much of the history of America in favor of the teachings of Judaism.

Many of our teachers were male, and most of those were rabbis. Mr. "D," our second-grade teacher, was an exception. In addition to not being a rabbi, he was distinguished by his lanky Ichabod Crane-like physique, the bounce of his oversized Adam's apple when he talked, and a short string of blue numbers tattooed on his forearm. Though no child ever said anything out loud about that string of numbers, each and every one of us knew they marked Mr. "D" as one of the thousands of Jews who'd escaped Nazi Germany's Auschwitz concentration camp. One of the lucky ones. Lucky, that is, if surviving that horror was luck. From a very young age, we were carefully taught that the Holocaust was worse than any boogeyman we could imagine and that it was never very far away. I've since been sickened to learn that the 1935 Nuremberg Laws that stripped Jewish Germans of their citizenship were inspired in part by the United States' Jim Crow era of laws that discriminated against Blacks.

At school, we ate kosher scratch-cooked lunches from pastel-colored plastic trays that always smelled like lunch from the day before. Mrs. Gardner, the lunch lady, was a squat grandmotherly woman with overbearing breasts beneath her full white apron. Her gray hair was always neatly tucked inside a fine mesh hairnet, and her cheeks were often rosy from the effort of preparing lunch for so many. She spoke with a thick Eastern European accent. Though I never saw a tattoo on her arm, I often wondered if she too was a survivor.

My parents kept kosher at home too, and even when I took up my place in one of the city's two public high schools, I was expected to do the same. The cool kids took their second- and third-hand Chevys and Fords to McDonald's for cheeseburgers or Big Macs. Both were forbidden by the rules of kashrut (keeping kosher), in which dairy and meat were not permitted in the same meal. Cheese (dairy) and hamburger (meat). Cheeseburger? Forbidden. I couldn't go to McDonald's.

The one exception to the rule of kashrut was when as a family we went out to dinner at the orange-roofed Howard Johnson's restaurant on Front Street. It was there that my dad broke the rules and thoroughly enjoyed an oversized platter of fried clams with a squeeze of fresh lemon and fries on the side. Shellfish are not permitted. I remember him smacking his lips in delight while my mother looked down her nose at him. Those fried clams were one of the few forbidden things my father allowed himself. That, and one can of Pabst Blue Ribbon beer after he mowed the lawn on steamy summer afternoons.

All my parents' friends were Jewish. Until high school, all my teachers and school classmates were Jewish. Friday nights my dad shepherded me and my sisters to the temple sanctuary's fourth pew from the front on the left for Sabbath services. On those Friday nights, my mother kept her eye on us from the choir loft behind a screened balcony above the pulpit. From that vantage point, she could not only see us, but she could also see every new hat and outfit sported by the congregation's women. Sunday mornings we attended Sunday School there too.

My mother entertained a monthly mah-jongg game with her girlfriends, who took turns hosting at each other's homes. When it was my mother's turn, there was always a freshly baked cake or homemade pie and a candy dish brimming with Brach's chocolate bridge mix. Sue and I would look over my mother's shoulder and feign interest in the game. All the while, we took turns nabbing chocolate-covered raisins and peanuts from the cut-glass dish on the living room end table.

On my parents' crystal anniversary, my mother harangued my dad into buying her a complete set of twelve etched-crystal water and wine goblets plus champagne flutes and cocktail glasses. Even to me as a nine-year-old, those crystal glasses seemed pretentious. My parents rarely drank alcohol or entertained. Until my mother died forty years later, those nearly unused glasses filled every cabinet in the back of the kitchen. I'm not sure they graced our dining room table more than a half dozen times. They've since taken up residence as heirlooms of the 1960s in my daughter's teak breakfront in South Florida.

On snowy winter mornings, still blanketed in my flannel pajamas, I'd lay quietly and listen for the crunch of my father's boots as he walked to the garage behind the house. He was an early riser and often headed to work at the Capital Bedding Company before 6:00 a.m., where, at the wishes of my mother and her family, he'd gone into business with his father instead of following his passion for a career of research and teaching in biochemistry. At the time, others valued a businessman more than a PhD-bearing college professor. When my father died at the age of sixty-three, only two years after retiring from the family business, he still had and read his subscriptions to chemistry magazines. It would seem my mother wasn't the only one who led a life of disappointment and regret.

In summer, Sue and I would stay outside until after dusk, capturing fireflies in jam jars filled with bits of grass and twigs. We didn't know their flashes were a mating dance. By the next morning, the flashes were gone. On those same hot, muggy East Coast nights, we would stand at the bottom of the attic steps in our baby-doll pajamas and let the oversized attic fan catch our tops like Marilyn Monroe's skirt on the steam grate.

We had plenty of good food and the most stylish clothes from the full-price rack at the downtown children's clothing store. Every spring we carted home brightly colored wool coats and white patent leather shoes for the Passover holiday. It was a picture-perfect growing up that was documented each year by hand-tinted photos of the three of us in matching dresses taken at the Olan Mills Studio on Third Street.

I grew up shrouded in a 360-degree circle of Jewishness. From home to the Jewish community center and Hebrew day school at Front and Vaughn. From home to Temple Beth El across the street. From home to William Penn High School. And from home to my best friend Geri's house. All less than a mile.

I thought every kid in every house in America lived like I did. There was only one harsh exception I knew of. The only thing others had that we didn't. The celebration of Christmas. On Christmas Eve at bedtime, until I was six or so, even though my parents shunned the Salvation Army bell ringers, even though we had no tree with silvery icicles and strings of cranberries, even though our house wasn't adorned with brightly colored lights, I secretly prayed to my Jewish God that Santa and his reindeer would arrive jingling on my family's roof at midnight and leave a small pile of sparkling packages wrapped in shiny paper by the front door. He never did.

I'm sure Freddy Burton had his own blank slate. I like to think his path early in life was more loving than mine. That he was wanted and that his family took pride in each of his accomplishments. In the one family photo of his I've seen, Freddy appears as a precocious toddler, his tiny head peeking out from under the edge of a dining table set for a large family gathering. I imagine the youngest children chasing one another around the table and the patriarch telling them to settle down. I imagine a lively conversation about summer holidays and plans for a bigger family reunion in the fall. I imagine the swapping of recipes and book titles and news of babies on the way and politics and classic bits of gossip about friends and neighbors.

That sort of family meal is one I've always wished for. Growing up in my family, dinnertime was a low-key, often silent affair. What was talked about had nothing to do with what was going on in the world and everything to do with the food on the plates in front of us. At our meals, my mother would report the caloric content of the food on each of our plates. I can now credit her for my own lifelong obsession with my weight and appearance. Whenever the subject of diets comes up, I'm one of few in the room who can tell you how many calories are in that brownie or slice of pie or sugar-free Jell-O you are about to eat.

On Thursdays, my mother often crowed about how fresh the flounder was. It was Thursday, she told us, the day the fishmonger brought his freshest catch of the day to the Third Street open-air market. I'm not sure it ever dawned on her that Thursday's fresh fish arrived for the Catholics—not for us.

As a teenager, when Sue wasn't there for dinner, we all knew where she was: playing tennis with her non-Jewish boyfriend until after dusk. My mother's clenched jaw and the less-than-subtle snarl that crossed her lips when she looked across the table at Sue's empty chair said more than words could have. I didn't need to be told that Sue was breaking the rules, and I knew there was danger there.

Unlike Sue, my growing up and coming-of-age were short on rebellion. I rarely broke the rules. I was never reprimanded in school for running in the hallways or called out for talking too loudly in study hall. I respected my teachers, turned my homework in on time, and earned nearly straight-A grades.

I wasn't perfect, mind you. In high school, I held hands with Billy Stout and loved the one-of-a-kind musk scent of his skin as we worked closely, side by side, in the third-floor office of the yearbook staff. Billy wasn't Jewish. As a freshman in college, when miniskirts shifted women's hemlines up from just below the knee, I cut five inches of wool off the bottom of three expensive, iconic Villager skirts and canned my cable-knit Suzy Long Leg tights for knee-highs. Soon after that, I spent ten dollars of my allowance on a pair of blue denim bell-bottom jeans at Jim's Army and Navy Surplus on Beaver Avenue in State College. I wore those jeans nearly every remaining day of my college career.

Against my parents' wishes, I changed my college major from chemistry to theater arts and refused to add teacher training to my curriculum. There was something more comfortable about taking on the character of someone else before an audience than grappling with the flaming Bunsen burners, periodic charts, boiling flasks, and too-tight unattractive goggles in the chemistry lab.

Getting into trouble for me as a twenty-something was hanging out with and making out with all manner of bearded, long-haired, non-Jewish young men who smoked cigarettes and passed around joints of illegal weed.

In the early 1970s, the violent scenes that were playing out between the police and Black men in the streets of West Philadelphia weren't even a glimmer on my radar screen. After I graduated from Penn State, I was perfectly content to live my life as it was intended to be. To make the natural progression from newly minted college graduate to little lady housewife with a modest second income from an office job that only required typing skills of forty words per minute. Given where my head was at the time, I can honestly say that even if I did know about the awful things going on in the streets of Philadelphia, I was far too removed to care.

When you sift and sort the bits and pieces in this way, sometimes the answer to questions about why you are who you are isn't so hard to find. For me and my sisters growing up, the codes were embedded. There was always the fear of "the other"—the Nazis of course, but also the others who did not share our faith—the Gentile *shiksas* and *shegetzes*—or the *schwarzes* with brown skin or the blue-collar workers with bad teeth who lived in a different part of town. There were a lot of "others" in the world to judge as something less. A lot of others to look down our noses at.

I wish I had heard the striking of the chisel when those bits and pieces were carved into my blank slate. I wish I had a tool to smudge them out.

"Fred Burton was basically a good youth who fell in with the wrong crowd," said DA Knauer in an interview with the *Inquirer* after Freddy's 1972 conviction in the Von Colln murder. "He came from an intelligent family who took an interest in him. He used to work with teenagers in West Philadelphia. His arrest for killing a park policeman in August was his first and only run-in with the law."

But Mr. Knauer wasn't there when Black men were harassed and brutally beaten by white police officers. Mr. Knauer wasn't in the back room when police commissioner Rizzo called all-out war on the Black Panthers. He wasn't there when Freddy and his friends vowed to protect their community against injustice and violence at the hands of the police.

I didn't know Wilhelm Knauer. But I don't think he could ever put himself in the shoes of a Black man in America in 1970. I don't think he could have understood what may have happened to change a "good youth" into a revolutionary because, like me, through no fault of his own, Knauer's blank slate was filled full of the privileges that come with being white.

"The system is designed to break us down and tear families apart," Freddy's fifty-four-year-old son, Freddy Jr., told a small crowd gathered to protest the 2020 police killing of George Floyd. "I was four years old when they took my father away. I grew up visiting him in a penitentiary. And he was there because he stood up for what he believed in and because the district attorney's office systematically built a fraudulent case against him. Slavery hasn't changed. My father has been in prison for fifty years. Fifty years is time enough."

XII
The Godson

In 2017, my first sweep through the Internet for Frederick Burton was enough to plant more than a seed of doubt in my mind about the fairness of his conviction in the Von Colln murder. The petitions for relief and Jonathan Gettleman's "Free Frederick Burton" web page still held a corner of my attention. I wondered if what happened between the police and the Black community in 1970 was not too far off from what had been happening recently between the police and the Black community. If a police officer could be acquitted of shooting an unarmed Philando Castile in the front seat of his car in Saint Anthony, Minnesota—for all to see from a video taken by his girlfriend inside the vehicle—then coercing false testimony from a witness more than forty years ago was small-potatoes injustice.

Whoever this Jonathan Gettleman fellow was, I was certain he knew things about Freddy that I didn't. Facts about the prison murders and the trial that had escaped me at the time. Nuances that might even justify the choice I made to convict.

Nine months after I stumbled on his web page, I was drawn to it again. Gettleman was a partner in Caballero and Gettleman, a small law practice on the corner of North Pacific Avenue and River Street in Santa Cruz. The firm specialized in criminal justice and civil rights. I clicked on and copied his email address from the contact information and sent him this message: "Mr. Gettleman, I served on the jury for Frederick Burton's prison-murder trial and have some questions I hope you can answer. Would you be willing to talk with me?" Whoosh. Sent. Then I went downstairs to reward myself with a cup of hot chamomile tea.

The teakettle was on the verge of its full-on air raid siren whistle when my phone rang. The Santa Cruz area code, 831, scrolled across my screen. I turned off the kettle's burner and listened to the phone ring three more times before I let myself touch the green icon.

"Hello."

"Is this Carol?"

"This is she."

"This is Jonathan Gettleman. I just got your email. It's amazing that you contacted me right now. We just got a copy of the immunity document that we've been trying to get for years. The immunity document that proves that Marie Williams lied. That in exchange for implicating Freddy, she was not arrested as a coconspirator."

I had no idea what Gettleman was talking about. This had nothing to do with the prison murders. "Mr. Gettleman . . ."

"Call me Jonathan." His voice was smooth and pleasant.

"Jonathan, I'm not sure I know what you're talking about." I wanted to get back to my agenda. "Mr. Gettleman, um, Jonathan, I've been troubled by the jury I served on for a long time—well, not every day, but especially when I get a jury summons. There was something that wasn't right in that trial, and I can't get my head wrapped—"

Gettleman cut me off in midsentence. "The problem is this. Each time we petition the court for a new hearing in his first conviction, the DA's office trots out the prison murders to bias the judge. Essentially what they've said is that whatever happened in the first conviction is irrelevant. This is the guy who killed the warden; he's a serial killer and a serial filer and he's wasting the court's time. They've consistently argued that there's no merit to his case. Now that we have the physical immunity document, this may be the first time we can tell our story to a judge. I've been looking for a way to separate the two cases," he continued. "Maybe you can help."

"Mmmmaybe. But I'm not sure how. I've got a lot of questions about the prison-murder case, and I can't find the answers." I spoke quickly, matching the lawyer's pace. I didn't want to be interrupted. "I'm wondering what you know about that. I remember having to choose between the testimonies of Leroy Taylor and Joe-Joe Bowen. I remember the instructions from the judge to the jury. He said that if Mr. Burton was present when the murders took place, he should be held guilty. That he should be convicted and sentenced as if he'd pulled the trigger himself or in this case stabbed the warden. What can you tell me?"

"Well, first, if those were the judge's instructions, they were incorrect. Do you have time to talk now?"

"Yes. And second, what?"

"Second, I don't know what really happened in the warden's office, but I do know Muhammed's truth about it."

"Excuse me. Muhammed?"

"Freddy dropped his slave name a long time ago. When he became a practicing Muslim, he took the name Muhammed."

Jerry's words of caution about networks of Muslim extremists bubbled up in my consciousness. The voice on the other end of the phone was coming at me like a fire hose. I tried to slow everything down. "Mr. Gettleman, I'm still not sure how I can help you."

"I think you can, but let me answer your question first."

"I'm listening."

The lawyer spoke again. This time at a pace considerably slower. "Joe-Joe and Muhammed were called to the warden's office to talk to the warden about more time for their Sunni Muslim prayer group in the community room. They didn't just show up. It doesn't work that way. They were searched twice before entering. No one could go into the warden's office without being searched. It would have been impossible to enter his office with a weapon of any kind. And no one traveled in the prison alone, and certainly not to the warden's office. There needed to be a witness to what happened there. It simply wasn't safe."

Just as Cecil Moore had presented his case in 1976, Gettleman told me that when the inmates entered Fromhold's office, Fromhold took two shivs from his desk drawer and threatened Muhammed and Joe-Joe with a transfer to the rival Nation of Islam Muslim cellblock.

At that time, members of the Nation of Islam had free run of the prison and were granted certain privileges by the prison administration in exchange for doing the warden's dirty business. "The warden might as well have declared a death sentence," continued Gettleman. And then he told me what Muhammed said were the precise words Fromhold spoke to the two men before hearing them out—words that were never repeated in the courtroom trial I witnessed.

I never knew Deputy Warden Fromhold, and I don't recall learning anything about him at the trial. All I know is what I've read in the news stories of the murders and his funeral, when four hundred people crowded into the church where he served as treasurer and a member of the board of trustees. If the pastor of his church who knew him well was correct, Bob Fromhold was "not a violent man, nor an arrogant man, nor a bigoted man. He was a good man, a man of noble motives, a man who loved and served his country, who lived for his family and for a work he regarded as his calling, not a job." If all that was true, could Bob Fromhold have said the following statement to the two prison inmates in his office requesting more prayer time?

"I'm not going to let you niggers run my prison."

The moment Jonathan Gettleman spoke those words, the moment I heard them, I felt a bitter taste in my mouth. The color of my memories of nearly fifty years before changed from tone-deaf black and white to screaming crimson. When I heard those words, I felt in my bones the cruel hate that had been seeping through the stone walls of Holmesburg for almost a hundred years. I could almost smell the smoldering disdain and lack of respect for humanity, the self-righteousness of a white man in power and the rage of two Black men without it.

The rest of Jonathan's version of the story was just as Joe-Joe told it. When the warden threatened the two men, Joe-Joe flew into a rage, grabbed the knives, and went after Fromhold. When Curran, who was outside the office, heard the scuffle, he entered the office and was mortally wounded. Freddy just froze.

Then the phone was silent. Gettleman was finished with his story. His narrative had played out like an Orson Welles radio drama. For me, calling those men niggers put that warden in a different class. Sure, he was law enforcement and he had a job to do. But using that word, addressing them as if they were something less than human, was unforgivable. At that moment, it didn't matter if the white warden was a loving husband and father. It didn't matter if he'd been recognized for his service in any number of ways or if he got a full-on military funeral with the folded flag handed off to his wife and children. What mattered was that if Gettleman's story was true, if Freddy froze, which is exactly what Joe-Joe testified to at the trial, he should not be held accountable for Joe-Joe's violent assault on the wardens.

"Joe-Joe was a real bad actor," Gettleman said. "Muhammed just wasn't that kind of guy. He came from a good, hard-working family. He had a job as a splicer with Bell Telephone. He was married with two kids and a set of twins on the way when Von Colln was killed. He wasn't like Joe-Joe Bowen."

Then there was one of those pauses in a phone call when you wonder if the call was dropped. I was afraid I was losing him.

"Jonathan, are you still there?"

"Oh, yes."

I doubled back. "What did you mean when you said before that the judge gave the wrong instructions to the jury?"

"I don't know exactly what the judge said. But if he did say what you remember, he was wrong. No matter what arcane law, you can never be culpable for a crime for merely being present when it occurred."

It was all too much to take in. "OK, Jonathan," I said, needing to change the subject, "tell me this. If you can get Freddy—er—Muhammed a new trial for his first conviction and if he's acquitted, how will he be free? He's still got the prison-murder conviction on the books."

"His sentence in the prison murders was harsh because it was the second conviction of murder. If we can get his first conviction overturned, he will have already served the maximum sentence—twenty years—he would have received for the prison murders. The judge will have to release him."

"How likely is that?"

"It's the only way I can think about it."

I can hardly know what's typical of life in prison, but there is no measure by which it is easy. Freddy served twenty-three years at Western Penitentiary, located on a floodplain along the Ohio River in Pittsburgh, Pennsylvania. According to Jonathan, in early January of 1997, six Western inmates dug a forty-foot-long tunnel from the prison's machine shop under its walls to a nearby road in an *Escape from Alcatraz*-style breakout. Several of the men were apprehended in Texas twelve days later. But Western was locked down for much longer. When Freddy, whose murder convictions and tenure at Western made him a de facto leader, approached the prison administration about ending the lockdown, he was transferred to a solitary confinement unit at Smithfield in Huntingdon County, then Huntingdon Prison a short distance away, then Frackville, then Camp Hill. With each move, he was placed in solitary again. There was a practice at the time of moving prisoners to another facility when they'd reached the legal limit of solitary confinement. When a prisoner was moved, the "solitary" clock started ticking again. That was one way so many prisoners were confined in solitary for so long.

In 2001, with his just-acquired law degree, Jonathan filed a writ of habeas corpus on Freddy's behalf and won Freddy his transfer out of solitary to Somerset Correctional Facility, where he remains today. All told, Freddy Burton has been transferred at least nine times to nine different prisons since 1970.

"And exactly how did you, in California, end up representing a man who was convicted of a crime forty years ago, three thousand miles away?" I asked.

"Muhammed," Gettleman answered, "is my godfather."

Just as I was beginning to think I'd reached the end of Frederick Burton's story, a forty-something white lawyer from Santa Cruz, California, added yet another leg to it. I couldn't make this up if I tried.

"Your godfather?"

"My parents were both lawyers. They represented Muhammed

and five other inmates who filed suit against the Pennsylvania prison system in 1977 for excessive use of solitary confinement."

Freddy was the lead plaintiff in that case, Jonathan explained. And he struck up what was to become a deep friendship with Jonathan's parents. They won their case, and for Jonathan, the baby boy born to the couple soon after, they named Muhammed godfather.

It turns out I wasn't the only one consumed by Freddy Burton's life. His life had also consumed the lives of two generations of the Gettleman family.

If this was a scam, I was falling for it. So when Jonathan suggested that he and his mother meet me in Davis, California, seventy miles away to talk about how I could help, I said yes.

XIII
Wicked Smart

It wasn't that many years ago that my boss described me in a performance review as "wicked smart." I'm not sure I knew exactly what that meant or how it made me such a phenomenal asset to the organization. But I took his statement at whatever face value I could. The first time I remembered hearing the term was when a character in the 1997 film *Good Will Hunting* used it to describe the self-taught genius that Matt Damon played. It was spoken with the South Boston missing *r*, "Wicked smaht."

When my boss described me in that way, I thought it was a respectable way to be seen, and I liked how it felt. Wicked smart. It was a pedigree I'd never given myself permission to have.

I had other identities growing up but none that felt as good on my skin when I tried them on as "wicked smart" did. In high school, I tried being a Twiggy-like anorexic before eating disorders became mainstream in American culture. Two years later, with two years of college under my belt, my weight skyrocketed from just shy of 110 pounds to nearly two hundred, when the earliest fad diets were the rage and too many believed obesity only happened to losers. Each of those personas disappointed everyone who cared about me and eventually disappointed me too. By the time I sat on that jury, my weight was carefully controlled at 125 pounds. At twenty-four years old, in one way or another, I was everything I was expected to be, and I've spent the best part of the rest of my life trying to live up to those expectations. Advancing from those earlier versions of myself to "wicked smart" felt like I'd taken three giant steps forward toward social acceptance, not to mention a much healthier existence.

People who are wicked smart solve complicated problems. They see through bullshit and lead others to decisions with reasoned, informed arguments. Arguments often powerful enough to move people off their single-minded frozen tundras. All good in my book. I see wicked smart as an intellectual gift influenced little if any by the emotions one feels in any given situation. Turn it on, stack the cards, and make way for getting what you want. It's an easy path out when emotions run high. For me, long ago, it just may have been the most effective way I could get out of the unbearable anxiety I felt stuffed away from the world I knew in that Holiday Inn. Long before my boss branded me with that well-suited moniker, I had those skills and I used them when my fellow jurors and I deliberated on Freddy Burton's fate. Perhaps I should have chosen more carefully how to use the gift I had.

XIV
Obituaries

On my sixty-fifth birthday, I was privileged with three life-altering events: (1) I became eligible for Medicare; (2) I became eligible for the senior discount at the local Ace Hardware store; and (3) I started reading the obituaries in the *San Francisco Chronicle* on Sundays.

On Sunday mornings at breakfast tables across the country, some people take their coffee black and reach for the sports page. Others take it with cream and sugar while reaching for the comics. I take my coffee with just a touch of steamed milk, flip through the paper, and slip out the section with the obituaries, or what the *Chronicle* euphemistically calls the "Life Tributes." For me, reading the obituaries is a way to vicariously live lives that are so different from my own. I love the way each life story is boiled down to some portion of a column or two and often accompanied by a photograph to fix the decedent's memory in the hearts and minds of everyone who knew them, as well as voyeurs like me.

Once I got the hang of it, I could find clues to each person's life story that made the weekly project completely satisfying. Anyone born near 1951, my birth year, gets my attention first. Then I peg some part of each decedent's identity through their surnames. There are the Tudonis and the Banduccis. The McDonoughs and the Murphys. The Goldsteins and the Shapiros. And if the cause of death isn't given in the first paragraph, there's often a clue in the last paragraph. That's where the family notes where memorial donations can be sent.

And then of course there are the pictures. I find it fascinating that the family who loses someone at 101 years old often chooses a photo of that person many decades younger. Some families post two photos. One from "then" and another from "now"—or almost now. For the men who served in Korea or WWII, the "then" photos often capture them in military uniform with full heads of hair. For women of the same era, it's the iconic double-victory-roll hairstyle and, in the occasional color photo, that brick red lipstick. What each photo depicts, regardless of the age at which it was taken, is a certain joie de vivre that is magnetic. Sometimes I wonder what picture of me would show that same love of life. As I'm not fond of having my picture taken, I'm not entirely sure there is one.

On one particular Sunday, it was Margy Wilkinson's Life Tribute that drew my attention. I never met her, and I hope her family will forgive me for using her story in this way, but I wish I'd lived the life of Margy Wilkinson.

According to her obituary, "The moment 17-year-old Margy Wilkinson was washed by a police-operated fire hose down the grand marble staircase of San Francisco City Hall, she knew this was the life for her." It was 1960 and Ms. Wilkinson was protesting McCarthyism. Soon after that, she drove three thousand miles from California to Washington, DC, to hear Martin Luther King's "I Have a Dream" speech. And soon after that, she was inside Sproul Plaza at UC Berkeley, being arrested while helping launch the Free Speech Movement. In 1970, she and her husband celebrated their wedding night by attending a "Free Huey" rally in Oakland for Black Panther leader Huey Newton. According to Margy's obituary, she and her husband supported the antiwar and Black Panther causes, and at her parents' dining room table in North Oakland, the defense strategy to free Angela Davis on charges of conspiracy and murder was organized. For most of her life, Margy Wilkinson fought for social justice, and she is rightly memorialized among dozens of others like her in a mural covering a boarded fence on the south side of Ashby Avenue between Harper and Ellis Streets in Berkeley.

I wish I had known Margy Wilkinson. I wish I'd protested the Vietnam War with her. I wish I'd traveled with her to the Mall in Washington. I wish I'd been as wise and sensitive to the needs of the African American community as she was when I was growing up. I wish I could have been her friend.

Margy Wilkinson spent a lifetime working for these things she believed in. I've only spent the last three years. I have a lot of catching up to do.

XV
The Keys

Freddy is sitting outside at a round metal table under a large red-and-white umbrella. Close in the background is a rocky shore. Gulls are hovering overhead; a few have landed in the sand looking for the errant french fry from a careless diner's lunch. There's a cool ocean breeze, and the smell of burgers and fries competes with the scent of salt air. The day couldn't be more perfect. Freddy looks like the last picture I saw of him on Jonathan's web page. An old Black man with a receding hairline and short lengths of salt-and-pepper dreads gently resting on his shoulders. He's wearing mirrored sunglasses and a white guayabera. There are sandals on his feet.

We're at the Lazy Days Restaurant on the Overseas Highway in Islamorada, Florida, halfway down Highway 1 from the mainland to Key West. My son, Josh, and I once ate amazing blackened mahi-mahi fish sandwiches with fries and coleslaw there. We both drank Coronas. The route from South Florida was lined on both sides by Jersey barriers brightly painted aquamarine—the work no doubt of an enterprising convention and visitors bureau or maybe Florida Department of Transportation civil engineers—or both.

Josh's and my destination that day was Seven Mile Bridge, which connects Knights Key in the Middle Keys to Little Duck Key in the

Lower Keys. There are two bridges there. A sleek modern one and the original bridge from the early 1900s that's been converted to a walkway for pedestrians and bicyclists. The old bridge ends precipitously after two miles with a view of the Atlantic Ocean where the water is the color of jade. Josh and I took selfies together there.

I can't imagine how Freddy got here. But he is. And there is a tall stack of pancakes with a slab of whipped butter in a pool of maple syrup on a plate in front of him. He looks so relaxed. So much like he belongs. I take the seat across the table from him. The table is so wide we're almost six feet apart. It is the first time we've met face-to-face, and I cannot be more nervous. What do you say to a man you sent to prison for life? What might he want to say to you?

My hands are sweating. My heart feels squeezed in my chest. Then I say the truest thing I can: "I really don't know what to say to you."

Freddy is listening in the shadow of the umbrella for what feels like a very long time. "Well," he finally says, "we're here, aren't we?"

When he raises his hands from his lap to reach for a fork, his two wrists are bound, locked together with a pair of rusty black wrought iron handcuffs. Terrified, I look down at his sandaled feet. They are bound too. His dark skin is ringed in their ancient rust. That's when I know it's a dream. When I open my eyes, I feel the weight on my chest pressing a deep sadness toward my throat. I want to cry.

I can't tell you how many dreams I've had about Freddy being free or almost free. Or about Freddy in prison breaking bread in the mess hall, where knives are no longer set at the table. About Freddy meeting with Jonathan and reviewing yet another presentation before another judge to ask yet another time to be set free.

When I don't dream, I imagine. I imagine leaping to my feet, weeping with joy when the judge tells him, "We're sorry for the pain we've caused you and your family for too long. You are free to go." Or the moment I stand off to the side watching as he exits the prison gates into the arms of his grown son and a gaggle of grandchildren and great-grandchildren who have never given up on his innocence.

XVI
The Declaration

It was early in the morning when Jerry and I pulled into the nearly empty parking lot at the Black Bear Diner on Second Street. The August heat in Davis already felt oppressive. We took a table for four, and Jerry started looking over the menu. I kept one eye on the door and one on my watch. We ordered coffee, and I nervously texted Jonathan that we'd arrived and were waiting at a table inside the restaurant.

The doubting Thomas in me wondered if I might be stood up. It felt strangely like the first date I had in 1967. Dave was a nice-looking Jewish boy. Our families were acquainted, and he needed a date for his high school prom. Somehow, when he spun the wheel, it landed on "nice Jewish girl" me. Under the circumstances, it might have been uncomfortable at best, especially the obligatory goodnight kiss after the dance on the brightly lit front porch of my parents' house. Until he arrived, boutonniere in his lapel and wrist corsage in his hand, I wasn't sure he would show up. But he did, and years later when he came out as gay, I understood that our date was probably far more unsettling to him than it was to me. Now his Facebook profile reveals a happy, relaxed gay man. Good for him.

Over long-distance phone calls between Southwestern

Colorado and California, my sister Sue and I used to search the Internet for long-lost high school heartthrobs and oddballs. Sue and I were only a year apart and knew most of each other's friends. I did the surfing on my end and sent her links to the ones that brought back the best memories. The hardest ones to find were the ones we wanted to find most. Her non-Jewish high school tennis-playing boyfriend never surfaced. And the first non-Jewish boy who told me he loved me must have died in Vietnam. There wasn't a single sign of him. As far as I know, Sue never reached out to anyone we found on Facebook. I know I didn't. When Sue died three years ago, Dave was among others who surfaced to send condolences. Desperate to hold on to her memory, I wrote to him and each of the others to acknowledge their kind thoughts. They were still alive. She wasn't.

"Are we still waiting for the others in your party?" perked the waitress, interrupting my memories of days gone by. "Coffee?" she asked at the same time, tipping her glass carafe toward my mug.

"Yes, please."

"Oh, yes." Jerry added as he pushed his mug toward the waitress. He was still studying the menu. I had my eye on the restaurant's front door.

I recognized Jonathan from his picture on his website. As he came through the double doors, I caught his eye and got up from the table to greet him. It was as if we'd known each other for a long time. Both of us reaching for a warm handshake. His mother, Eleanor, had a small gift bag in her hand and a carton of a dozen eggs. I reached out and shook hands with her too. She handed me the bag with a small Ball jar of homemade strawberry jam and the eggs. I was beginning to feel at ease.

"It's so nice to meet you." Her voice was smooth and husky at the same time. "The eggs are from our chickens. They will be fine in the car until you get home."

As they looked over their menus, I looked over them. Eleanor was a stunning woman with sparkling blue eyes and freely styled shoulder-length salt-and-pepper hair. I figured her age in the seventies, but I swear she looked like an older version of the debutante she must have been. Another notable thing about her appearance? She was wearing blue jeans, a cool cotton shirt, and a lovely strand of pearls. Only a woman of supreme confidence wears pearls with jeans to breakfast with strangers in a small-town restaurant dedicated to bears. I liked her. Jonathan had her eyes, but that's where the family resemblance ended. I guessed the rest of him was handed down to him by his father.

The smell of home fries and bacon pulled me back to the present. Jonathan leaned in across the table and started to talk. He talked about an upcoming hearing. He once again told me the story of how the police brutally coerced Marie Williams to name Freddy as a conspirator in the Von Colln murder. He recited horrific details about how she was held against her will in a room at the police station for sixteen hours. How she could hear shouting and the cries of her husband being beaten in the next room while handcuffed to a chair that was bolted to the floor. How she was threatened with arrest as a coconspirator herself. How the only way to get home to her children and out of earshot of her husband's tortured cries was to agree to name Freddy as a conspirator. And she did.

Soon after, more clearheaded, she hired a lawyer and then took the Fifth Amendment, refusing to testify against Freddy. The only way the police could force her testimony was to grant her immunity from prosecution as a coconspirator and take the death sentence off the table for her husband.

Though she later admitted under oath that she was coerced to make the statement, it was too late. The cards were already stacked against Freddy, and no one was listening anymore. The truth was an afterthought. Despite the countless attempts to get the evidence of the immunity document from the DA's office, it had taken decades to get it. I could only imagine that someone in the DA's office made a mistake when they handed it over. The failure of the system was lost on them. It had all been so long ago.

The DA's case against Freddy was twofold, Jonathan explained. First, the evidence of the immunity document was time-barred, they said. There was a statute of limitations, and it was too long after the conviction to introduce such evidence. Second, Jonathan told me again, that in the minds of the DA's office staff, the Von Colln case was conjoined with the prison murders like Siamese twins joined at the head. The two cases could never be separated.

Jonathan knew I had my doubts about the fairness of Freddy's conviction in the prison murders. He wanted me to make a declaration to be added to his brief. He wanted me to ask that the court focus its attention on the Von Colln murder without any consideration to the prison murders that followed.

"Let me draft something for you," Jonathan said. "You can look at it and see if you're comfortable with it. You can put your own words to it. It will be yours. Do you think you can do that?"

My French toast and bacon had gotten cold. All of our breakfasts had barely been touched. The waitress was on her third round of coffee refills, and I put my hand over my cup. "Yes, I think I can."

Until then, Eleanor had spoken few words, giving the floor to her son. When I tentatively agreed to help, she smiled warmly and offered a simple, "Thank you."

XVII

The Nemesis

I write at some length about the Von Colln murder because it was the first time that Freddy Burton found himself in the wrong place at the wrong time. His conviction of that crime landed him in prison with a life sentence that de facto landed him in the warden's office at Holmesburg the day of the murders.

Before his conviction, Freddy was a community activist. One of several young African American men in his West Philadelphia neighborhood who formed the Black Unity Council, a spinoff of the local Black Panthers. The council dedicated itself to improving the quality of life in their predominantly Black neighborhood and to resisting the police brutality that was prevalent under the administration of Police Commissioner Frank Rizzo. Rizzo later served two terms as the city's mayor.

In the decade between the 1970s and 1980s, if Philadelphia's African American community had one single nemesis—one ultimate enemy with the power to destroy them—that would have been Frank Rizzo backed up by his cartel of law enforcement officers, none of whom were held accountable for the brutality they inflicted on the city's African Americans.

At nearly six foot three and two hundred pounds, Rizzo was a bigger-than-life figure with the well-deserved reputation of a might-makes-right public servant. He charmed his constituency of white working-class Philadelphians and shamelessly menaced liberals and progressives who found his tactics heavy-handed. From the day he entered the city's police department as a twenty-three-year-old rookie, he was a force to be reckoned with. As a young cop, he led raids on Center City strip joints and coffeehouses where neighbors complained about beatniks going in and out at all hours. As a devotee of the FBI's J. Edgar Hoover, he made himself the enemy of the city's Black revolutionaries, who objected to his abuse of power and the police force's open brutality against their community. As mayor, he opposed the desegregation of Philadelphia's public schools and thwarted the building of low-income housing in predominantly white neighborhoods. For all this, in 1999, he was memorialized with a ten-foot-tall bronze statue in front of Philadelphia's Municipal Services Building.

Rizzo wasn't a premodern Christopher Columbus or a nineteenth-century Jefferson Davis or Stonewall Jackson. He didn't commit genocide or fight to protect the South's right to own enslaved people. Frank Rizzo was a twentieth-century postmodern historical figure who was given free rein from Philadelphia's city fathers to lead a regime of social injustice against African Americans who still live today. He was a nemesis to all of them and to all others who opposed him.

I moved to Philadelphia a short time after graduating from college. I was twenty-three years old and busy with a new job shuffling paperwork in the international shipping department of my brother-in-law's family moving-and-storage company. Compared to my hometown of Harrisburg, Philadelphia offered a big-city life. I loved walking to the streetcar stop and riding to work from Center City to North Philadelphia. I loved the independence of living in my small studio apartment on Juniper Street. I loved the future I envisioned for myself there.

What little I knew of Frank Rizzo and his tactics was just a sideshow. I didn't know that three years before, in 1970, Officer Von Colln was mortally wounded in a shooting at the Fairmount Park guardhouse or that police had fingered Freddy Burton and fellow members of the Black Unity Council for the murder. I didn't know that hundreds of police officers had swarmed Freddy's neighborhood and terrorized his family. I didn't know that Freddy went to the local precinct with his attorney to find out why his home had been invaded by law enforcement. I didn't know that he was immediately strip-searched and arrested for the Von Colln murder.

In the late 1960s and throughout the 1970s, law enforcement's coordinated assault against Black revolutionaries was playing out in cities across the country. One of the more public examples was the 1969 murder of Chicago Black Panther chairman Fred Hampton. Just eight months before Freddy Burton was arrested for Von Colln's murder, Chicago police officers fired more than ninety bullets into Hampton's apartment, killing him and another fellow member of the Panthers and wounding several others. More than ninety bullets from law enforcement and only one documented bullet from the residents of the apartment. At the time, the killings were characterized as justifiable homicide. Twelve years later, in a civil lawsuit filed by the survivors, the courts awarded the plaintiffs nearly $2 million. Today, many believe Hampton's killing was a cold-blooded assassination coordinated by the FBI.

In 1969, when Fred Hampton's apartment was riddled with bullets, I was safely asleep in my bed after an evening school dance in which I was among the musical performances. Dressed to the nines in a blue-and-silver-striped evening gown and silver pumps, I held the mic close to my lips and sang "Cockeyed Optimist" from Rodgers and Hammerstein's musical *South Pacific.* At 4:00 a.m., when Fred Hampton's body was peppered with bullets, I was probably dreaming about exotic fish and living coral in clear water with white sand. Safe and beautiful.

I never knew Frank Rizzo, but I have to believe he was something more than just evil. I imagine him in the breakfast nook of his Chestnut Hill home on Crefeld Street, sipping his morning coffee and smelling the ink and newsprint from the daily paper. With his salt-and-pepper hair slicked back, his burly features look gentle behind his glasses as he reads "Dear Abby" to his wife, Carmella, and they laugh together. Carmella is modestly fingering the pearl necklace he'd given her for their anniversary the week before. And I can imagine him in his brown fedora and trench coat kissing her goodbye at the front door as he leaves for work. "Have a good day, Franny," Carmella says. "I love you." And like gangland heroes Jimmy Hoffa and Tony Soprano, Frank Rizzo leaves the comfort of his family and home to do his dirty work.

I can imagine him in 1970 after work, taking a seat at his favorite table at the Vesper Club in Center City, rolling a Partagas cigar between his thumb and forefinger, and sniffing the dark wrapper's sweet smell. As he strikes the match to light up, a tall sturdy Black man is taking long steps across the dining room toward his table. The Black man is his bodyguard, Anthony Fulwood. Rizzo would have been less than pleased to have his happy hour at the club interrupted, but with his open palm, he gestures toward Fulwood to approach the table. Fulwood leans in to whisper in the commissioner's ear.

Officer Francis Von Colln of the city park police has been shot five times at the Cobbs Creek guardhouse, Fulwood tells him. Von Colln is dead. Three other officers have been wounded.

Fulwood might have held the commissioner's chair for him, carefully taken the unlit cigar from the ashtray, handed the commissioner his hat and coat, and walked with him toward the club's front door.

"I've got business to attend to," Rizzo tells the tuxedoed maître d'. "I'll see you soon. My best to your wife."

Despite his pleasantries to the maître d', the commissioner's hackles are raised. The murder of a police officer and the assault on three others is a personal affront.

I never knew Frank Rizzo, but I know this much to be true: From his command post in city hall, in retaliation against the suspected offenders, he ordered his men in blue to raid Black Panther headquarters, to force those inside into the street, and at gunpoint demand that they strip naked like enslaved people on an auction block. He invited photographers to stand by so that his triumph would be recorded, played, and replayed in newspaper headlines across the country. And it was.

"The way to treat criminals," he once told a reporter, unashamed, "is *spacco il capo*. Translated from Italian: 'Break their heads.'"

I never knew Frank Rizzo, but I imagine that Carmella Rizzo found a way not to care about what orders her Franny gave from behind his desk from nine to five. At the end of his day, Carmella simply fluffed the cushions on the damask sofa and readied her husband's first, or maybe second, Jack Daniel's of the evening.

XVIII
My Truth

Submitted to the Court of Common Pleas January 16, 2019

IN THE COURT OF COMMON PLEAS PHILADELPHIA COUNTY
CRIMINAL TRIAL DIVISION

COMMONWEALTH OF PENNSYLVANIA,	DECEMBER 1970 NO. 1004, 1005, 1008 CP-51-CR1210041-1970
FREDERICK BURTON,	DECLARATION OF CAROL MENAKER

I, the undersigned, do hereby declare as follows:

1) My name is Carol Menaker. My date of birth is ████████ My address is ████████████.

2) In the summer of 1976, as a twenty-four-year-old woman, I served on a sequestered jury in Mr. Burton's Holmesburg prison case at docket number Commonwealth v. Burton, September term,

1973 Nos. 0041, 0042, 0043, 0044. My name at the time was Carol Michaels.

3) Today, I have deep misgivings about the jury's verdict in that case. Further, I believe I was wrong to find Mr. Burton guilty.

3) For that reason, I am deeply troubled by the district attorney's repeated attempts to influence this court by parading Mr. Burton's conviction of the prison murders as evidence against his present petition to overturn his conviction in the Von Colln murder case. I believe the decision in the case now before this court should be based only on the evident facts of the false testimony of Marie Williams and nothing else.

3) Many times in the last forty-plus years, I have had genuine doubts about my decision to convict Mr. Burton. Two years ago, I began my own investigation of the crime in an attempt to find answers to questions that had remained unanswered in the trial proceedings. With that information, I have come to understand that my decision to convict Mr. Burton was gravely misguided by:

a) The traumatic experience of being sequestered. From early on, I felt I was being held against my will with no recourse. I should note that I was not the only juror who felt that way.
b) The conflicting testimonies of Captain Taylor and Joseph Bowen.
c) The lack of testimony by Mr. Burton himself.
d) And my lack of understanding of Judge Prattis's instructions to the jury.

4) While the testimony revealed that Mr. Burton was indeed present in the warden's office at the time of the murders, his participation

(1) according to the testimony of Captain Taylor was vague and (2) according to the testimony of Mr. Bowen was nonparticipatory. I have never believed Mr. Burton personally stabbed anyone or aided in the stabbing of anyone.

5) My understanding of Judge Prattis's instructions was that Mr. Burton's presence in the room at the time of the stabbing of the wardens and Captain Taylor was evidence enough to convict him of second-degree murder. In 1976, with the information I had, I voted my conscience based on those instructions.

6) In 2018, through my own investigation of the prison murders, I came across the website of Mr. Burton's counsel, in which he described his family's forty-plus year effort to gain justice for Mr. Burton in the Von Colln case.

7) Please note that I shared the above information via letter to Mr. Krasner's office and to Patricia Cummings, head of the Conviction Integrity Unit, some months ago. I have not received a substantive response to that letter.

I declare under penalty of perjury pursuant to the laws of the Commonwealth of Pennsylvania that the foregoing is true and correct. Executed this 16th day of January, 2019, in [redacted].

[redacted]

Carol Menaker

XIX
The Storyteller

It's 1982 and I'm sitting in the Gregory Hall basement office of my advisor in the University of Illinois's master's program in journalism. Bob Reid's desk and the bookcase behind it are stacked with papers and books and less-than-orderly file folders from years of teaching and grooming fledgling journalists like me. Bob has made it his mission to keep all four wheels of democracy on solid ground. To reinforce the powers of the fourth estate by feeding talented young writers into the nation's pool of journalists. Conversations with him are always through a thick cloud of smoke that his own eyes, squinting through the magnified lenses of his glasses, seem to have become accustomed to. The ashtray on his desk is always full of butts, and his ivy-covered basement window is yellow inside from years of nicotine inhabiting this space.

I love journalism school. I love how formulaic and easy it is to tell a good story. I love gathering information from lots of sources and making sense of the who, what, where, why, and how of every story I've ever written. And I never wanted to disappoint Bob Reid.

Today, Bob is chagrined at my news. Once I've completed my thesis, I'll be looking for a job in public relations. I'm almost thirty-one years old, I tell him. I'm married and have a young son. I'm really not in a position to take an entry-level job with a local newspaper and write obituaries or cover city council meetings to climb up the ladder. PR pays more, I tell him. Wouldn't you rather someone with integrity make inroads into that world?

"You're too good at this, Carol," he told me. "I hate to see you sell out."

I remember leaving Bob's office disappointed. Disappointed that he didn't approve and disappointed in myself for not meeting his expectations.

Though I only occasionally regretted my choice to go to the dark side, as he saw it, I've never forgotten Bob's words or his passion for doing what he thought was the right thing. I will always be grateful to him for preparing me to be the most honest person a public relations person can be.

Over forty years, I've taken those skills to colleges and universities, where I wrote recruitment materials and student and alumni profiles of the best and brightest. I've taken those skills to agency work for competitive high-tech firms, where the clients were never happy with anything less than 100 percent market share. Those were the years that Bob Reid's voice spoke loudest to me.

When the dot-com boom busted and I was summarily laid off from the agency, I was relieved to go back to the world of nonprofits, where I pitched stories for an under-the-radar multiple sclerosis research foundation. The Myelin Repair Foundation had good, honest, important stories that truly mattered, and I was good at engaging reporters to tell those stories. I only pitched the stories that had real value. And I credit Bob Reid's voice in my ear for helping me to do the right thing.

XX
A Bold Pledge

For decades, Freddy's adopted family of attorneys, the Gettlemans, never lost hope. From what they've told me, neither did Freddy. In 2018, their hopes blossomed when the citizens of Philadelphia elected a district attorney whose campaign pledged far-reaching criminal justice reform. Larry Krasner came to the DA's office with thirty years of experience as a criminal defense and civil rights lawyer and public defender. He was known for his zealous pursuit of police misconduct. But most important, Larry Krasner promised to investigate unfair convictions that had resulted from police coercion or prosecutorial misconduct. Philadelphia County has the second-highest number of people incarcerated per one hundred thousand residents. Second only to Oklahoma County in Oklahoma. For Krasner, there was much work to be done.

Once in office, Krasner summarily fired a third of the old guard staff and surrounded himself with as many as he could who shared his belief that the DA's office had some mea culpas to make. He created a separate Conviction Integrity Unit to investigate unfair convictions. In the first year, hundreds of incarcerated inmates from state prisons across Pennsylvania set their pleas before Krasner's staff. For the first time in the decades of Freddy's incarceration, the Philadelphia

District Attorney's office appeared to have a change agent at the helm. A man who on paper would put justice before politics.

Jonathan Gettleman was banking on DA Krasner to open the gates of Philadelphia's criminal justice system so Freddy's appeal could be heard. If Krasner was to walk the talk, Freddy's case was the perfect vehicle.

Despite the many attempts to reach him directly, Krasner never responded to Gettleman's appeals. Instead, Freddy's case was being handled by Krasner's subordinates. It seemed in their eyes that any alleged unfair hearing in the Von Colln case carried no weight in the face of the historic prison-warden murders. Despite my greatest hope, my declaration to the court wasn't enough to hold sway with Krasner or his minions.

But Jonathan had not tried to use the media to get Krasner's attention, and this was something I had some expertise in. My research into Freddy's cases brought any number of reporters to my attention who were interested in the subjects of mass incarceration and false convictions. And Jonathan was agreeable to my trying to engage one of these reporters to investigate and report Freddy's story. Freelance journalist Gail Gerson is one of those reporters. She is an excellent reporter and writer whose stories are published in high-profile media outlets. Outlets that would get Krasner's attention.

I'd spent too many helpless days looking for ways that I could help shed light on Freddy's situation. Right or wrong, I felt like I owed him more than goodwill. If I had the means to do that, I should and I would.

So with Bob Reid's angel on my shoulder, I sent Gail Gerson an email in which I described Freddy's situation in three short paragraphs. I asked her to let me know if she was interested in knowing more. To be honest I hadn't the faintest hope that I could get her attention. Solid reporters like Gail are hard to connect with. They might get dozens of pitches while they are in the middle of writing something they're already committed to. And they often have reliable sources that they are more prone to respond to. So when my phone rang only a few minutes after I'd hit the send key, I wasn't as prepared as I would have liked to answer her questions. We spoke for half an hour, and I sent her off to talk to Jonathan. As PR people like to say, we had her on the hook. But reeling her in to investigate and publish a story would be far more challenging. In the end, after staying in touch with us for a short while, she disappeared. No more email replies. And no story. When Jonathan wins Freddy his freedom, I will let her know. That will be a groundbreaking story worth telling.

XXI
Luck

By most measures, I am one of the luckiest people on earth. I live in a storybook, gingerbread-trimmed, mortgage-free Victorian in Nevada City, California. Nevada City is a Northern California gold rush town. In the 1850s, thousands of poor Cornish miners came here to get rich, and a small handful of entrepreneurs came to get richer. The Empire Mine in neighboring Grass Valley was one of the oldest, largest, deepest, and richest gold mines in California. In the hundred or so years it was in operation, it produced 5.8 million ounces of gold. Today, there is a sign on one of the mine's outbuildings that says in 1849, that gold was worth $20.67 per ounce. In 2019, an ounce of gold was $1,583.60.

Just off the town's Broad Street exit from the freeway, visitors are greeted with the archaic remains of a water cannon, one of many sprinkled about town that were used to strip away the hillsides and bare the land for hundreds of underground mining passages. Nevada City is where, in 1870, Lester Allan Pelton built the first commercial Pelton wheel in the city's iron foundry. Pelton's design employed as many as fifty spoon-shaped buckets on two sides of a six-foot-diameter spinning wheel. It became the industry standard for the hydroelectric power needed to run the mines.

Today the Miners Foundry offers the rare combination of a sought-after wedding venue, a collection of gold-mining artifacts, and a cultural center hosting weed-scented dance parties and oldie-but-goody artists doing late-in-life tours.

If time travel were possible, one might find the threesome of Norman Rockwell, Nathaniel Currier, and James Merritt Ives having breakfast with the town mayor at Java John's coffee shop on Broad Street. Together they would be planning the dozens of picture-perfect parades and street fairs and art walks and farmers' markets that attract thousands of tourists on holidays and weekends each year.

The town is most famous perhaps for its Victorian Christmas celebrations, in which townspeople saunter about the three-block downtown in period costumes singing carols in four-part harmony. A single horse-drawn carriage with a top-hatted coachman clip-clops through neighborhoods, transporting to another time couples and families bundled up to their chins in heavy plaid woolen blankets. If the December weather cooperates, a light dusting of snow swirls among the period gas-lamp streetlights that are part of freezing this town in a time not quite forgotten.

Nevada City also hosts the nation's only Constitution Day Parade, in which townspeople dressed as US presidents and their first ladies march through the town center between E Clampus Vitus members' cardinal-red Jeeps and fez-hatted Shriners riding motorcycles too small for grown men. It is a town where no one seems to wonder why the church bells toll nineteen times every weekday morning at 7:20. And it is a town where one should not be surprised to see the likes of *Andy of Mayberry*'s Aunt Bee, Opie, or Barney Fife in line at the post office.

Every day, Jerry and I eat sweet, buttery steel-cut oats for breakfast from the recipe of a café owner in Oakland. Or smoked salmon, scrambled eggs, and brown bread to cement our memories of the breakfast we ate on the sunporch at No 31, a hotel on Leeson Close in Dublin. Ireland is one of several faraway places where we've vacationed in recent years. We buy whole, local, organic food at the high-priced co-op to supplement the seasonal shares we buy from a local farm and discounted "Tony's Picks" of red, white, and rosé at Grocery Outlet. I take a Pilates class on Wednesday and a yoga class on Sunday, and I ride with the local bike club on Tuesdays or Thursdays. I have one, two, three levels of boost on my e-bike to kick ass up the town's formidable hills and adaptive cruise control on my two-year-old Subaru Crosstrek. For me, at nearly seventy years old, that's having it all.

As you and I know, nothing is perfect. The gold rush era that brought such phenomenal riches to so many in this small town nearly obliterated the Nisenan tribe of Native Americans that hunted, farmed, and lived on the land. Chinese immigrants taxed as foreign miners fell victim to violent attacks in the mining camps. Today, this place I live in is lily white. Of the 3,068 residents, less than 1 percent are Black. And for the most part, despite the apparent charm, Black people are rarely seen among those who vacation here.

I can't forgive the oversized QAnon flag I pass on one of our favorite cycling routes. I can't forgive the white teenage bullies who chased a Black woman and her young child out of a local park. I can't forgive the two dozen white men who confronted and taunted an equal number of Black Lives Matter demonstrators marching through downtown's main street. I can't forgive that the small local synagogue must hire off-duty policemen on the High Holy Days so that those who attend can pray in peace and not fear. And I can't forgive the gangs of aging, ponytailed men on motorcycles who patronize a bar on the main street where I'm told Confederate flags hang from the walls.

Jerry and I moved here from the San Francisco Bay Area to retire. I don't miss the traffic or the McMansion luxury homes sprouting from the lush hillsides or the world that thrives on venture capital and exit strategies. But I do miss the richness that comes with ethnic, racial, and cultural diversity. If you asked me, I'd have a hard time explaining how I ended up in a place that doesn't seem to welcome it.

For the last three years, few days have passed that I haven't thought about Freddy Burton. I've spent hours on the Internet printing pages and trying to keep them in some order on my desk and more hours reading fiction and nonfiction about the Black experience in America. I've looked for simple ways to tell others what I'm learning and why it is so important. Ways to organize the telling of the story in the time it takes for an express elevator ride to the Top of the Mark sky lounge in San Francisco. Ways to tell the story before the listener's eyes glaze over and the subject changes to the weather or this week's police blotter that is published in the *Union* newspaper, or whether I've seen the local community theater production of *Cabaret*. Though it was not my intention, it seems Freddy Burton, in the Somerset Correctional Facility seventy-five miles southeast of Pittsburgh, has become part of my consciousness. Sometimes his presence is a tiny pinprick of light in the back of my mind. Other times, when the news brings yet another hate-filled crime against African Americans, his presence weighs heavier on my chest than the town carriage's thickest woolen blankets.

XXII
Silence

Sometimes I crave silence so much I want to scream. In every waking hour, I'm subjected to the dull buzzing of fire planes in concert with the chopping of helicopter blades. Both making their rounds over the city, looking for that tiny swirl of smoke spiraling up from the woods. I don't need to be reminded that it's fire season or that where I live could be another Paradise, California. Two years ago, eighty-five people died there in a fire so hot it melted the tires and bumpers off the cars that didn't make it out. Many of those who survived drove from their homes through high walls of flames on both sides of the only roads out. Many of those, not knowing if they would survive, left messages on the cell phones of loved ones, telling them goodbye and that they loved them.

Then there's Jack across the street, a pinto pit bull mix who can't resist barking his sharp commentary at every person who walks by, with or without a dog. Taking Jack's lead are Casper and Dodger and the three fancy Italian greyhounds who live next door to Jack that ping off one another whenever Jack kicks up some dust. Sometimes I wonder if there are more dogs in Nevada City than residents.

There are the too-wide-for-the-street garbage trucks that roar in like a Boeing 747 on the tarmac at 6:00 a.m. on Tuesday mornings, clanking their automated hooks into the six cans that sit in front of our house, emptying their contents with a screech, then dropping the cans on the blacktop with one, two, three, four, five, six loud thuds.

And then there's the constant drum of bad news from Jerry's ritual 5:00–7:00 p.m. dive into TV broadcasts that remind us of all that's wrong in the world. After the news, there's always an hour or so of his soul-searching self-talk that closes out with him asking me: "And what do you think?"

I know if I answer that question there will be more noise, more conversation, about solving the problems of homelessness or health care or climate change, or stopping a pandemic that I wish I'd never lived to see. So I stay silent. Sometimes I'm not sure how I managed to choose a life partner who is a best-in-show news junkie, and I'm embarrassed to say how often I chastise myself for that oversight.

But the loudest and most persistent noise of all is the rumble in my head about Freddy Burton. It's a heavy backdrop to the other annoying everyday clamor that surrounds all of us, all the time. It holds my attention and demands that I do something—anything—to undo what I did and do what I can to never let it happen again to anyone else.

The worst feeling there is about this particular rumble in my head is that it feels like no one is listening. It's become part of idle chatter between me and my friends, and worse, between me and Jerry. Being asked "How's your book coming?" has come to mean the same as "How are you?" Many people ask but few really care about the answer you give. So I stay as silent and as polite as I can. And that makes me want to scream too.

In June 2020, Quiet Parks International, a nonprofit dedicated to putting natural quiet within reach of humans, certified the world's first

Urban Quiet Park near Taipei, Taiwan, in Yangmingshan National Park. And according to One Square Inch of Silence, founded by acoustic ecologist Gordon Hempton in 2005, possibly the quietest place on earth is in the Hoh Rain Forest at Olympic National Park in the state of Washington, GPS coordinates N 48.12885°, W 123.68234°. "Silence is not the absence of something," writes Hempton, "but the presence of everything."

I can hardly imagine what silence might sound like to my ears.

It's July 28, 2020. In twenty-one days, Freddy will have a hard-earned Post-Conviction Relief Act hearing before a judge; he'll sit in a chamber inside the Juanita Kidd Stout Center for Criminal Justice, just four hundred feet from city hall, where he was tried so many decades ago. How ironic that this structure was named after the same judge who sentenced Freddy for the Von Colln murder in 1972 and declared the mistrial in his first prison-murder trial.

For the first time in all those years, a judge will hear testimony about the police coercion that led to the false testimony of a key witness in his 1972 trial. For the first time, the same judge will hear about the district attorney's deliberate effort to hide that evidence from Freddy's attorney and the attorneys of each and every one of his four codefendants.

Jonathan Gettleman has his ducks in a row. If this is ever going to happen, it will happen now.

"Freddy tried to live the American dream," Jonathan's father, Paul, once lamented. "And the American dream turned into an American nightmare."

I'm counting these twenty-one days. Twenty-one days until I log on to my computer and click on a Zoom link to watch the hearing from my desktop in California. This time it's not the twenty-one days

I was held as a juror in the downtown Holiday Inn. Instead, it's the twenty-one days until Freddy might be vindicated. He deserves that much, even if he doesn't go home. When all that happens, maybe the noise of everyday life won't seem so loud.

XXIII

Unspoken Rules

It's an unspoken rule: When you walk or hike trails, don't pick the wildflowers. Don't take the multicolored rock that looks like the face of a chipmunk or the egg of a Steller's jay the color of a blue sky on a sunny day. Growing up in Pennsylvania, there was a myth that it was illegal to kill a praying mantis. And anywhere in the United States, the Bald and Golden Eagle Protection Act prohibits all non-Native Americans from taking or possessing an eagle feather. I've asked myself more than once how anyone would know if you violated these rules, unspoken—and maybe spoken. I wondered if a neighbor who saw the errant feather on your desktop would report you to someone. Like who? The county sheriff? Like who?

When my son, Josh, was a toddler, I preached the "Don't Pick" rule about wildflowers. There were many near our house in Central Illinois. But the Queen Anne's lace drew him like a magnet. He squealed their name every time we came across them. "Keen Anne's lace!" His *Q*s were simple *K*s then. "Keen Anne's lace!" I'd try to distract him from picking two or three of the hundreds of flowers in our path. But the truth is, there were days when despite the warnings I'd internalized throughout time, we did twist off a handful the size of his tiny fist, take them home, and set them on the dining room table in a glass full of water. *It brings him such joy,* I'd think, *and they are so lovely.*

Yesterday, when I took my daily trek up American Hill Road, I came across a small patch of Humboldt's lilies. Five blossoms hung like lanterns from two stems. If you've never seen them, the sight of them can take your breath away. They're not like other lilies. Their maroon-speckled, pumpkin-colored flowers hang upside down. Six upward-curled petals fold up on each flower, exposing six stamens with tiny hammer heads on their tips. I've learned that, unlike me, they are native to California.

Some years back, the first time I saw them on the trail, I wanted to take them home. It was the same two stems with the same five blossoms. I remembered Josh and the talk we always had about the "Keen Anne's lace." So I stopped briefly to take a picture in my mind and walked on. I've done the same every July when they spring from the greenery in that same spot by the side of the road. I witness them like old friends and walk on.

But these days, my walks are rarely peaceful. In my head, I am still sifting through newspaper clippings, printouts of court petitions, and images of racial violence against African Americans at the hands of the police and others in which no one is held accountable. I am still trying to assemble Frederick Burton's story. Inside my head, I can only hold a fraction of the rage that African Americans must have felt—must feel. I've become edgy and irritable. I've stopped talking to Jerry about each clue I uncover. I keep it inside, hoping for the day I might connect all the dots and reconcile who broke what rules and why.

It's a sunny spring day. From where I stand, I can see in the distance a shimmering domed Greek Revival-style building. The building is surrounded by what looks like quaint, solid structures that could have been an early American city. A river runs along its banks. The maples and sumacs and birches are lush with buds, and the air is easy to breathe. I am inside a pavilion that cloisters hundreds of six-foot metal coffins suspended vertically above my head. *What is this ghostly place, and why am I here?* It could be a dream, but it isn't. The Greek Revival building on the landscape below is the Alabama State Capitol. The town is the City of Montgomery. The river is the Alabama River, where in the 1800s steamboats deposited enslaved Africans from Mobile and New Orleans to auction blocks in the city's center.

I am at the Equal Justice Initiative's National Memorial for Peace and Justice. I am here to witness one of America's darkest and most hidden hours of history. Each stark monument is imprinted with the name of a county and state: Homer County, Mississippi; Union County, South Carolina; Lafourche Parish, Louisiana; and many more. Below the name of each county are the names of African Americans who were brutally murdered in public executions without the benefit of even the disingenuous justice Frederick Burton received. The memorial honors 4,400 African Americans who were killed—lynched from trees and gallows and viciously beaten in all manner of racial terror. Thousands of African Americans who fell victim to America's timeless affair with racism.

Like the deep piles of worn shoes on display in the Holocaust Memorial Museum in Washington, DC—all that is left of millions of massacred Jews and others in Nazi prison camps—these heavy steel coffins hanging overhead are symbols of the worst in humanity. The pain they carry could shatter your heart into a million tiny pieces.

I am not alone in this mausoleum. Around me are intimate clusters of the descendants of those memorialized here. Each small group is wearing matching T-shirts printed with the names of their loved ones and the dates of their executions. It would be hard to feel anything but deep sadness for their losses.

Earlier in the day, I'd seen pictures in the museum downtown of these lynchings and the cruelty of the slave trade. I wonder what blind eyes took those pictures and what unspoken rules kept them silent.

I have to step outside. I cannot stop thinking about the 1970 newspaper photo of seven young Black men—Black Panthers—hands in the air, stripped naked against a brick wall. The resemblance to what I am seeing in this small Southern town on a river is shaking me to the core. The only difference between the two is just over eight hundred miles as the crow flies South and one hundred years, plus or minus, on the Gregorian calendar.

At an afternoon ceremony in a small auditorium at the edge of the memorial, EJI Executive Director Bryan Stevenson offers a stirring speech. His words, rhythmic like those of a Southern preacher, bring tears to my eyes. "Each of us is more than the worst thing we've ever done," he tells a group that fills every seat in the small auditorium. A sprinkling of *amens* rises from the assembled. In that moment, I know for certain that whatever Freddy Burton did or didn't do that landed him in prison for life, he is far more than the worst thing he ever did. He is a good man with a loving family who has stoically suffered injustice for too many years. He has more than paid his dues and deserves to go home.

I'd chosen to make this trip with my ex-husband's sister and niece, both of whom I hadn't seen or heard from since 1991 when Mark and I divorced. It was a reunion to be remembered as the three of us leaped across the decades, filling in the blanks that had been missed through such a long separation. Whatever we'd shared in our past lives, on those two days in Montgomery, Alabama, we shared something much more profound.

When the visit to Montgomery came to an end, I arranged with Patrick, the Black cab driver who picked me up at the airport on my arrival, to drive me back to the airport for an early morning departure to California.

"How was your visit, Miss Carol?" he asked, making me feel too much like Miss Daisy.

"I wish I'd had more time to see the rest of Montgomery," I told him. "It looks like a lovely town to visit."

"When you come back, Miss Carol, I'll take you over to the bridge in Selma. I bet you'd like to see that too."

Patrick was right. I would like to see the bridge. The Edmund Pettus Bridge where, in 1965, when I was only fourteen years old, peaceful civil rights demonstrators led by Martin Luther King Jr., John Lewis, and others were assaulted by the City of Montgomery's police. The march on that bridge was a landmark in the civil rights movement.

I hope I do get back to Montgomery one day, and when I do, I hope to see Patrick, whose hospitality made the trip that much better.

XXIV
In Memoriam

In 1970 there were 637 murders committed in the state of Pennsylvania. Three hundred and fifty-two, more than 55 percent of them, were committed in Philadelphia. On Saturday, August 29, of that year, forty-three-year-old Sergeant Francis Von Colln was one of them. Midmorning, alone at his desk in the Fairmount Park Cobbs Creek guard station, he was shot by an intruder. The uncoiled black cord of his phone's receiver hung off his desk by his large torso. Upside down on the desktop was his officer's cap. Next to the cap, a half-full glass bottle of Pepsi Cola. Officer Von Colln, a seventeen-year veteran of the police force, had just returned from a two-week vacation at the shore. According to the newspaper, he left behind a wife and four children, ages sixteen to twenty.

In 1973, the year forty-seven-year-old Warden Patrick Curran and fifty-one-year-old Deputy Warden Robert Fromhold were slain at Holmesburg Prison, the state recorded 754 murders, 57 percent of which were committed in Philadelphia. Warden Curran left behind a wife, four children, a duck named Taffy, and a German shepherd named Thor.

My insight into the injustices that have shuttered Freddy Burton in prison for fifty years come from my personal involvement in Mr.

Burton's prison-murder conviction and the efforts to seek justice in his conviction of the murder of Officer Von Colln. They come from my belief that African Americans have been consistently discriminated against in our country's formal and informal systems of justice. But it would be disingenuous of me to disregard the tragedy for those who knew Francis Von Colln, Patrick Curran, and Robert Fromhold. Three men who did the jobs that were expected of them and were honored for doing so. Freddy Burton's consistently unresolved dilemma with the justice system doesn't make what happened to these three men right. They deserved to live long, full lives with their families and those who loved them. From the Hebrew, *Olav ha-sholom*. May they rest in peace. May they all rest in peace.

XXV
Grounded

Though I couldn't be more grateful for the two exceptional children Mark and I brought into the world, our marriage was a sixteen-year stumble around the country for one job after another that Mark didn't seem to be able to hold on to.

Our first stop was Huntington, West Virginia, in the western foothills of the Appalachian Mountains. It was the furthest south I'd ever been. There we watched the bicentennial Fourth of July fireworks fizzle over the Ohio River. I don't know what the city is like today, but even then, in 1976, it felt frozen in the 1950s. There was still a drive-in A&W, and local entertainment was going for the half-price-drinks-and-appetizers happy hour at Club Pompeii at the local Holiday Inn. There, a poor imitation of a Disneyland volcano erupted on the hour. When the town's first Burger King opened in 1977, a line of hungry locals wrapped around an entire city block. And, oh, the local men favored string ties, something I hadn't seen since watching any number of cowboy TV shows as a kid.

At the time, Huntington was a place where Jews and Black people were few and far between. The closest kosher butcher was 146 miles away in Cincinnati. I hated living in Huntington, and I started hating Mark for taking me there. When the town was established, it was the terminus of the Chesapeake & Ohio Railway. Moving to West Virginia advanced our marriage toward a terminus of a different sort.

Our next stop was Miami, Florida, where I was first introduced to flying cockroaches and winter holidays with eggnog around a swimming pool. It felt exotic. It felt too hot. All the time. I started a master's program in special education, a career I thought would be transferrable if we were to move again. Two courses in and eighteen months later, I was pregnant and we were packing up to move to the Midwest, where Mark had taken a job with a city there.

Mark was and is gifted with intelligence. But sometimes it seemed that left little patience for those who were less gifted. People don't like being looked down on or treated as if they are somehow less than others. I'm not sure he understood that. I am sure that was part of the reason he couldn't hold a job for more than two years.

In Urbana, Illinois, in a house perched at the edge of a corn field, I fell into the rhythm of most married couples I knew. Our son, Josh, was born there in 1980 at a Catholic hospital where the nurses were so swamped with deliveries he birthed himself. Mark worked and I struggled as a stay-at-home mom, meeting occasionally with a playgroup of moms and babies. It simply wasn't satisfying to me. The other moms had somehow all mastered the skills of motherhood and babyhood and to me seemed to be deliriously happy about it. I always felt like I was getting a failing grade.

Eighteen months later, when Mark resigned from his job, I enrolled Josh in the Children's Center Day Care for forty hours a week and started a master's degree in journalism. I resolved to not leave there until I finished my degree. Mark would just have to figure something else out. Ten unsatisfying years later, we separated. Mark moved out to an apartment, and I stayed in our suburban tract house with our now two children in the southeast corner of town. My daughter, Elyse, was four years old. Josh was eleven. These days, Mark and I chat on birthdays and exchange stories about the lighter days of our marriage. I am happy for him that he is contentedly remarried.

In 1950s America, vowing for better or worse, for richer or poorer, meant a life sentence. By 1990, the world had changed. I had more friends who'd been abandoned by husbands or who had abandoned them than friends who were still in their first marriage. Women had careers and assertiveness training and day care and incomes of their own.

Through all this, I don't think I thought about Freddy Burton once. All I could have known was that he was still in prison somewhere in Pennsylvania. I didn't need to know anything else.

XXVI
An Icon

In 1955, when I was four years old, the brutal death of Emmett Till came to epitomize the kind of racial terror that lay in wait for other African Americans in the land of the free. Fourteen-year-old Till was visiting relatives in Mississippi when he and his cousin skipped church and found their way to Bryant's Grocery and Meat Market on Money Road to buy candy. White shopkeeper Carolyn Bryant accused the young boy of flirting with her. Several days after the incident in the store, Mrs. Bryant's white husband, Roy, and his half-brother, J. W. Milam, kidnapped young Emmett at gunpoint from his great-uncle's house, then beat and mutilated him before shooting him in the head. His body was discovered and retrieved from the Tallahatchie River three days later. One month after that, an all-white, all-male jury acquitted Roy Bryant and J. W. Milam of charges of kidnapping and murder. Sixty-two years later, an aging Carolyn Bryant told author and historian Timothy Tyson that she falsely testified against Till.

In my lifetime, I have seen *Life* magazine photos of Black high school students in Birmingham, Alabama, being stung by high-pressure water hoses wielded by law enforcement officers; I know countless others have seen these photos too. We have seen the same white uniformed police officers siccing vicious German shepherd dogs on activists who protested in that same city. We have seen images of hundreds of unarmed Black protestors being beaten with billy clubs and sprayed with tear gas on the Edmund Pettus Bridge.

We saw Rodney King, a Black man, brutally beaten by white Los Angeles police officers and saw those who committed the crime acquitted. In 2019 in Monroe, Louisiana, police body camera video showed a white Louisiana State trooper bludgeoning a Black motorist with a flashlight while the victim screamed that he was not resisting. Three weeks before, troopers from the same agency punched, stunned, and dragged another Black man before he died in police custody on one of Louisiana's rural back roads.

And in the age of livestreaming on the Internet, the entire world has seen violent assaults on Black Americans peacefully protesting these unconscionable acts of brutality. All of these are acts of violence by law enforcement officers who are sworn to protect us—all of us.

The only way to deny this unaccounted-for persecution is to not understand or to refuse to understand what racism is and how white America has allowed itself to be blind to the myriad obvious and subtle ways it plays out in our nation's towns and cities and states every single day and to inherently believe that people of color are less human and of less value than others. I do not believe that. Not for a second.

According to the House of Representatives Bill H.R.35, the Emmett Till Antilynching Act, passed by the US House of Representatives in February of 2020, nearly two hundred antilynching bills had been introduced into the US Congress during the first half of the twentieth century. No single one of them passed.

Between 1890 and 1952, seven presidents petitioned Congress to end lynching. Between 1920 and 1940, the US House of Representatives passed three strong antilynching measures that failed to gain Senate approval. It wasn't until early in 2022, nearly one hundred years after the first antilynching bill was passed in the House, that the US Senate unanimously passed a bill that criminalizes lynching and makes it punishable by up to thirty years in prison. Change is indeed slow.

All of this is the stage set for my encounter with Freddy Burton so long ago in a courtroom in Philadelphia City Hall. And it's the same stage set for Freddy's continued failed efforts to get justice from a criminal justice system that is blind to the double standard it has maintained for the life of this republic.

Freddy Burton has lived almost fifty years of his life in prison because he was fighting to survive as a Black man in America. From the day he was born and raised in a loving family, his path in life—his life story—was in so many ways defined by others. The feeling that comes over me as I think about this is rage. Rage that the odds were set against him from the day black-skinned Africans were taken off the ship, placed in pens, slicked with grease, and sold to the highest bidder.

Once again, it is July in California. And once again those five lilies greet me on the trail. This time, I look around me, bend down, and put my thumb and forefinger around the stem that holds three blossoms. As I twist the stem, the flowers dust my wrist with a cloud of orange pollen. I am breaking an unspoken rule. A hundred feet down the road is a patch of starched-white Queen Anne's lace with the dot of tiny purple petals at the center. There are at least a dozen of them, and there are dozens more patches on the trail ahead of me. I twist off two of those stems too and assemble the contraband bouquet in my fist. I walk that bouquet another mile and a half home and set it in a glass full of water on the dining room table.

XXVII
A Pandemic

It's May of 2020. The world is reeling from a pandemic in which nearly a hundred thousand Americans and countless others around the world have died. We have been masked and distanced from our friends and family for nearly ten weeks. Our stores, our parks, our theaters, our restaurants closed. Our towns, from New York City to the small town in Northern California where I live, have shut down. And more Americans than ever at any time in the history of our country are out of work. All of this disproportionately falling on the backs of people of color.

Then, as others look on, a brave young woman at the corner of East Thirty-Eighth Street and Chicago Avenue in Minneapolis records a white police officer pressing his knee on a Black man's neck for nearly nine minutes until that man, George Floyd, takes his last breath. Mr. Floyd repeatedly told the officers he could not breathe. We can see it. We can hear it when he calls for his mother as his life is being taken from him. Not one of the four officers present heeds his cries.

The world is roiling from this unspeakable injustice, from this cold-blooded murder, and I sit with tears in my eyes and a heavy heart knowing that as a white person, fifty years ago, I could have made a different choice.

As I understood it at the time, by law, Frederick Burton's conviction of second-degree murder was legitimate. But if that was the law, it was wrong, and that's where the buck stops. It stops with me and others who have spent their lives going along to get along. It stops with me and others who too often believe in the Golden Rule as long as "thy neighbors" are white. It stops with those who follow a set of life rules that take into account those who "have" and not those who "have not."

On June 4, 2020, in response to Black Lives Matter protests against the murder of George Floyd, the City of Philadelphia removed the three-thousand-pound statue of former police chief and mayor Frank Rizzo—the man who led such aggressive policies against all people of color and who drove the chariot in the 1960s and '70s that led to unfair convictions of any number of African Americans, including Frederick Burton. Let that symbolic and long-awaited measure not be the end of the story.

XXVIII
The Hearing

This should be the end of the story. August 18, 2020. Fifty years after Officer Von Colln was shot. Fifty years since Marie Williams was offered immunity against prosecution for testifying that Freddy Burton was part of a plan to blow up a guard station in Fairmount Park where Von Colln was killed. Forty-eight years since, on the witness stand, she recanted that statement. And forty-eight years since Freddy was convicted of murder and sentenced to life in prison.

On this day, a dozen people from across the country are logged in on Zoom to bear witness to an evidentiary hearing in Philadelphia that has been too long in coming. Each of us is linked to Freddy Burton in a different way. A thread of hope for honesty, transparency, and justice binds us together.

I am one of these people. Quietly sitting in my home office where this story has found its way to the page. Waiting and watching. Observers have been asked to turn off our video and audio to avoid distraction. In the image I see, the courtroom looks small and colorless. Not like the imposing hallowed space I recall. Jonathan Gettleman has traveled to Philadelphia from California to make the case of his lifetime. He is suited up and black-masked against the threat of COVID-19. His aging father is seated near him.

On this long-awaited day, Jonathan's mission is to prove to the court that Marie Williams lied and that the DA's office knew she lied and further obstructed justice by hiding her immunity document from Freddy and his attorney. Jonathan takes his seat and adjusts the microphone so we can hear. He has an air of preparedness. He is ready.

The judge looks kind. My age. Maybe a little younger. A single long salt-and-pepper braid hangs gracefully down her back. Her small diamond drop earrings catch the courtroom's light. She is wearing the traditional black robe. Head and shoulders. It's all I can see of her on my laptop screen. I'm sure she's some white child's grandmother.

Two years ago, this judge threw out the murder conviction of a forty-eight-year-old African American man who'd served twenty-eight years in prison for a crime he did not commit. The evidence of his false conviction? Prosecutorial misconduct, an ineffective defense, and a witness's false testimony. My heart is warmed toward her for her courage. And my sometimes-flagging hope for Freddy makes way for the best to come.

The first words she speaks are colored with the Philly twang. If you ever heard it, you'd know what I mean.

My respect for the prosecutor is less sanguine. She is the only one in the courtroom whose video is turned off. I've chosen to believe she doesn't want to be seen. Her tone is condescending, and she speaks to witnesses cruelly, as if they are children who have broken the rules. Her steely voice is filling the courtroom and vibrating along every foot of broadband between Philadelphia and Northern California. It feels like she has something to prove. My take is that the good old boys in the Philly DA's office put a woman on this case so that if she doesn't win, it will be because of her gender.

If I was a good, mindful person, I might think the prosecutor has a hearing impairment. Perhaps that would explain why she shouts. I've been told by others who know courtroom behavior better than I that some lawyers choose to shout to make their case. I can recall Cecil Moore being one of those. But I'm feeling no kindness toward today's prosecutor, who for reasons I don't know chooses not to be seen, and I'm only slightly embarrassed about my cynicism. I feel tired and despairing about everything the world has to offer me right now.

The climax of this story should have been the testimony of seventy-four-year-old, twice-convicted murderer Freddy Burton. The testimony no one heard in 1972. We can all see Freddy. He's Zooming with us from an empty room at Somerset Correctional Facility in Western Pennsylvania, where he's been an inmate for nearly twenty of his forty-eight years in prison. He is being broadcast from a camera in the prison to a monitor in the courtroom to the monitor on my desktop. His image is blurred by the vast space between us. He too is masked.

The temperature in California is nearly in the triple digits. Fires are burning. I'm wearing shorts and a T-shirt; my go bag and a plastic tub with our cat Lucy's essentials are in the back of my car in case we need to evacuate. In the prison in Western Pennsylvania, where I'm told the indoor temperature is kept cool to slow the prisoners, Freddy is wearing a thick black sweatshirt. Across its back are branded the large white bold capital letters *D O C*. The Pennsylvania Department of Corrections believes it owns him.

It's hard for me to comprehend that this hearing is not about whether or not Freddy participated in the murder of Officer Von Colln. I know that. Jonathan has explained it to me more than once. But that's what we should want to know. That's what I want to know.

Instead, its focus is on the relative truth of Marie Williams's testimony and the relative truth of Jonathan's contention that the DA's office stacked the deck against his client. All of this has been boiled down to a legal argument about process. There is no compassion. No heart. Just words.

And here is the prosecutor again, power belting her questions and repeating them relentlessly to an old man who somehow has retained his dignity in prison after nearly five decades. I imagined this moment for a long time. I imagined it from the time I met Jonathan Gettleman and his mother at the Black Bear Diner in Davis and learned of their unwavering conviction to make things right for Freddy. The moment I would see Freddy's face after so many years.

When the courtroom camera revealed the link from the prison, I couldn't take my eyes off the old man with the two strings of his white face mask hanging down the sides of his face. Foolishly I thought I'd recognize the young man from the courtroom so long ago. I didn't. The person I saw was a stranger.

This should have been the climax. Freddy testifying after all these years. Clearing up any confusion about whether or not he was involved in Von Colln's murder. The first time he was in the wrong place at the wrong time.

As I watched, glued to my computer screen, I again imagined him being free. I imagined the moment when this fair and kind and forgiving judge would make a heartfelt apology for the state of Pennsylvania for unfairly convicting him. For taking his life away. "We're sorry, Mr. Burton," she would say. "You are free to go."

But that didn't happen. None of it happened. I left the Zoom meeting room after six days of hearing testimony. Six days of listening to the prosecutor's painfully scowling voice pummeling everyone within earshot. Six days of bonding with the invisible others on that

Zoom call. Listening. Watching. Waiting for the world to turn upside down so an old man could spend the last years of his life at home with his family. But for me, just as in the six days I sat in judgment of Freddy so long ago, that ending didn't come.

Instead, the prosecution has been granted six months to submit a brief, and Jonathan will have time to rebut it, and the judge will then have time to consider all of it, and Freddy Burton will have time to wait, again. Though there may still be a win for Mr. Burton, I'm not sure I can wait any longer.

I've been consumed with understanding the events of Freddy Burton's encounter with the criminal justice system for the last three years. From the end of the prison-murder trial in 1976, I wound my way back to the beginning of this story in 1970, when Freddy was arrested for the Von Colln murder. For countless hours, I've sat at my computer and searched for new clues. And even though I thought I'd scoured the universe for every last detail, it seems new clues appear from time to time. The Internet is like that.

At times, I've felt as if all of this was a fool's errand. Trying to string together pieces of a story in a straight line from point A to point B. There has been no such path in this journey for me, for the Burton and Gettleman families, or for so many others whose lives have been touched within its universe. In fifty years, the pieces have fragmented and blown into the wind like the soft, errant whispers of pollen from those Humboldt's lilies on the trail in late summer. Just so many infinitesimal specks of pollen in so many directions, next to impossible to collect. Even the stories within the story have become choppy and disconnected. At times there is doubt. At other times, certainty.

The events that led to Marie Williams's statements and testimony that placed Freddy Burton within a circle of individuals who planned and executed the murder of Francis Von Colln make their own twists and turns.

Freddy Burton was only one of five African American men tried and convicted of the Von Colln murder. One of those men, who became known as the Philly Five, was Hugh Williams, Marie Williams's husband. When he was taken into custody near the scene of the murder, police brought Marie to the station for questioning, where she identified several of her husband's friends that she overheard planning to blow up a police station near Sixtieth Street in Philadelphia. Freddy Burton was not one of the men she named. Several days later, she was again brought to the police station and asked again about Freddy Burton's involvement. It was in her second statement that she named Freddy. As a result of that statement, Freddy Burton was arrested and charged with murder.

Soon after, Attorney General Fred Speaker and District Attorney Arlen Specter sought a joint petition for Marie Williams's immunity in exchange for her testimony against Freddy and the others. Marie opposed the request for her own immunity and responded with the letter below to Philadelphia District Attorney Richard G. Phillips. The letter was written on October 14, 1970, about two weeks after the Von Colln murder and two years before Freddy's trial. It was released to Freddy and his attorney thirty-one years later in 2003. The immunity document itself was finally disclosed in 2018.

Marie Williams, now deceased, can no longer speak for herself. But her words in this letter say more than I can ever say about the injustice that she and each of the men convicted of the Von Colln murder may have faced. She writes:

Mr. Phillips (District Attorney),

I heard in court the other day, and Mr. Rutter (Ms. Williams' attorney) has also told me, that you are going to have the Police come to my house again and try to make me testify. You know the Police have already been at my house many times and have made me go lots of places, including the Police Building at 8th and Race and the Courthouse at 20th and Montgomery. You also know that one time the police took me and my children to the courthouse at 20th and Montgomery and would not let me speak to my lawyer so that he could protect me and my children. In fact, you were in the Court yourself that day and you did not tell him that you were keeping me upstairs in the courthouse. In addition, you will not let me or my lawyer see any of the statements the Police forced me to give at the police station the day they had me and my husband there.

The purpose of the leeter[sic] *is to tell you, once and for all, that I will not testify on behalf of you, the Police Department or the Commonwealth in any case. Your detectives forced me to give untrue statements at the Police station at 9th and Race Streets by threatening me and my husband, by not allowing me to telephone any of our family or friends, by not allowing me to talk to a lawyer, by keeping me in the police station when I wanted to go home, and so forth. The statements that they forced me to give about my husband, Fred Burton and the others are all untrue and I will not repeat those lies again. So far as I know my husband nor any of the others I know had anything to do with the crimes they have been charged with. Please do not force me to come to Court again.*

Respectfully,

Marie Williams

Some days I feel as hopeful about Freddy Burton's freedom as I did during the last exhausting days I was pregnant with each of my children. Each day I'd wake up in the morning and wonder if that would be the day I'd bring into the world the tiny human I'd nurtured so close to my heart for so many long months. When that day came, I could feel joy and love and relief. I could feel as if I had opened a new door in my life and the first door in the life of my new child. Yes, on some days, that's what thinking about justice for Freddy Burton feels like to me. When the judge hands down her ruling and releases him from prison for time served, it could be his last day in prison. It could be his first day in a new life.

Other days I feel like I've reached the end of a hopelessly long trail. I feel shame that the thin thread of hope that Freddy Burton may one day be free or at least have the false narrative that the system created for him put to rest is beyond my grasp. I am a very small part of fighting a system that has been cultivated and sustained for centuries. It's hard to beat and harder to not feel defeated.

But when I look to the Gettleman and Burton families, I know my despair is misplaced. They've been at this a lot longer than I have, and their faith that justice will be served is resolute. The word *defeated* doesn't exist for them. And it's spelled out concisely on a hand-printed poster on the wall in Jonathan's ten-year-old daughter's bedroom in Santa Cruz. She is now the third generation of the Gettlemans to carry the torch for justice. The sign reads: *Muhammed is going to walk out of prison a free man and we are going to be there to see it. NOW!*

"Though he is confined in prison, Freddy is one of the freest, most unbound people I know, including at times myself," Jonathan wrote me in an email. "Justice has chosen to not open its eyes, which is unforgivable because if it did, it would see a beautiful, peaceful man who wants to spend his few remaining years in the presence of his loved ones. Instead, it keeps its eyes closed and only sees an imaginary role it cast for him."

XXIX
How Many Words?

How many words does it take? *How many words does it take?* To tell a story that will break your heart? Or a story that will mend your heart? Or a story that will make you angry or fearful or frustrated or enraged or sad? Or joyous? Or forgiving? Or jealous or proud? A story that will make you feel wiser or better or different? How many words?

Outside the temperature is sizzling hot. The sound I hear is what I fear are thousands of cicadas crackling high up in the trees. I learned to hate cicadas from a classroom assignment in my ninth-grade biology class. It was complicated because I had a deep crush on my biology teacher. As a fifteen-year-old pubescent, I would have done anything to earn his smile or even a nod of approval from him. The assignment was to collect insects, preserve them, and affix them to a white block of Styrofoam inside an empty cigar box. It was a sort of competition among my classmates. More insects, better grade. Bigger or more intimidating insects, better grade. Better grade in my case seemed essential.

I remember that finding the cigar box wasn't all that easy since no one in my family except my Uncle Marvin associated with the less-than-genteel habits of cigar smokers, and he lived one hundred miles away. But I must have found one. And the pins. Straight pins, as I recall, that I pierced through the thick exoskeletons of at least a dozen and a half bugs. The worst was the cicada. It was the biggest. I doubt I preserved it in my little jar of alcohol. Handling it made me jumpy. I had the crazy idea that at any moment this apparently dead, two-inch-long critter in the order Hemiptera might open its leaded-glass-like wings, turn its red eyeballs toward me, and then, I don't know. I feel spooked just thinking about it. But it was the crunch when I put the pin through its tough outer body that set the stage for my lifelong fear, and I should say disgust, of cicadas.

I'm sure I was clueless about the sounds they made. And why I attribute the interminable clicking I hear under those trees to them, I can't be sure. It is like the sound of charged high-tension electrical wires. But there are no wires. Just trees. Cedars and maples and oaks and redwoods and sugar pines trying desperately to shade us and keep us cool. Trees crackling along the Cascade Trail, where the only thing cool is the water running through a centuries-old ditch that enterprising mine owners constructed to power their water cannons and blast away the forests. On this crushing afternoon, the sound is eerie. I should have known its aura portended something I didn't want to hear.

It was news from Jonathan. A week ago, ten months after Freddy Burton stood before the kind-faced judge and told his story of what happened in the days leading up to his arrest for the Von Colln murder, and ten months after his godson, Jonathan Gettleman, delivered a one-two punch into the heart of the Philadelphia DA's case, the judge ruled. Freddy Burton's petition to reverse his conviction was denied in a one-sentence order with these two words: *untimely* and *meritless.*

The judge. The masked woman with earrings that sparkled, who appeared thoughtful and engaged for the six days of that hearing.

Who honored the opposing attorneys and refereed the jabs leveled at Jonathan by the prosecutor. What a stunningly believable performance she gave. A performance that persuaded those of us who watched that she was listening.

I was fooled. We were all fooled to have placed our faith in someone who, when even a modicum of compassion could have prevailed, chose cruel and heartless words designed to destroy all hope that there will ever be justice for Freddy Burton. Even if that justice only means an admission that the narrative the system wrote for him is false. Two words: *untimely* and *meritless*. Even if some interpretation of some law guided her to that decision, I want to know what that law is and I want to change it. It's all broken.

I weep as I tell my son, Josh, and text other friends of this news.

"They couldn't let go of the prison murders," Josh tells me.

"I know that," I tell him. "And I was the only one who could have changed that, and I tried. The only one alive who could have changed that."

"But your book, Mom, that's your testament. That tells the story, and that will change the narrative, and the judge and the courts and the DA can't stop that."

For a brief moment I feel a sliver of relief. But I say to myself, *Easy for me. It's too easy for me.* When it's too hot outside, I am free to enjoy a cool air-conditioned house. I am free to drive down the hill to Roseville and load my shopping cart with anything I want at Trader Joe's. Or visit the designer at Crate & Barrel about replacing our twenty-plus-year-old sleeper sofa with another that will fit through a too-narrow doorway. And I am free to stop at a local natural-foods restaurant in Auburn thirty miles from home, eat a vegan wrap, and drink an iced-cold golden milk. Free to do all those things in one single day.

All the while, Freddy Burton is inside a prison in Somerset, Pennsylvania, where he warms himself in a bulky black Department of Corrections sweatshirt. Where he eats from a metal tray. And where he may even still be in solitary to protect him from COVID.

The feeling of powerlessness is deep and painful. I can't imagine what the Gettleman and Burton families feel. I want to be with all of them in Philadelphia in Fred Burton Jr.'s living room serving some version of the Jewish custom of shiva, in which the family and loved ones of a deceased join in their grief and share memories of the one they lost. In Fred Jr.'s dining room where potluck casseroles and salads and brownies and iced glasses of sweet lemonade and the earthy smell of beer grace a table that should have been dressed for a celebration. Where Freddy's infant grandson, Assad, is babbling in his high chair and everyone who enters the space is hugged or high-fived in spite of COVID.

No, Freddy Burton is not dead. But the state of Pennsylvania and the City of Philadelphia have ruled that he will never be free when no one can be certain of exactly what is the worst thing he's ever done. Isn't fifty years in prison enough?

"Sometimes the hardest work is recognizing the limits of our control," writes Jonathan to those of us who have traveled on some or all parts of this journey. "This man, Freddy Burton, who is known to those who love him as Muhammed," writes Jonathan "has been affirming, high-spirited, and ready to keep fighting." And so is Jonathan. They are the courageous ones. And they yet again will file an appeal.

Sundiata Acoli, a former Black Panther member, has been incarcerated for forty-eight years for the 1973 murder of a New Jersey State trooper. It's August 2021 when *The Guardian* reports that a coalition of Black police officers have filed an amicus brief with the New Jersey Supreme Court in which they describe Mr. Acoli's continued imprisonment as "an affront to racial justice."

The group writes: "Mr. Acoli has spent more than half of his life in prison cells the size of a parking space, including nearly twenty years as a senior citizen . . . He should be granted parole."

In a written communication with *Guardian* reporter Ed Pilkington, Acoli wrote, "I am an eighty-four-year-old man who's been imprisoned since age thirty-six for almost fifty years, who now poses a threat not even to a flea, let alone public safety. My sentence is obviously too long. I am rapidly disintegrating before my family and friends' eyes."

The first time Acoli came up for parole in 1993, he was told he'd have to wait another twenty years before he could reapply. In 2014, a three-judge panel ordered his release, saying he was no threat at all. That ruling was overturned by the state supreme court. He is now appealing again to the New Jersey supreme court, which is expected to consider the case later this year or early next.

According to the National Registry of Exonerations, there have been 3,299 exonerations since 1989. Three thousand two hundred ninety-nine false convictions overturned. The number of "years lost" that exonerated defendants spent in prison for crimes they did not commit is more than twenty-eight thousand. And innocent Black defendants served a majority of those years. More than half of those exonerated received no compensation from the government entities that stole their lives away. The leading cause of these false convictions, reports the registry, is misconduct by government officials. And finally, in the United States, only 1.5 percent of prosecutors' offices have established conviction-integrity units to investigate the thousands of false convictions that have been made under their watches.

So what do we do? Where do we go? Whose shoulder do we cry on? Whose arms do we yearn to be embraced in? Whose minds do we open? And how do we do it? When does this story end, and are there ever enough words to tell it?

XXX
Lessons

I'm floating on an inflatable vinyl mattress in Oregon Creek. It's a favorite swimming hole of ours seventeen miles north of our home near Camptonville. Creeks and rivers and other natural bodies of water have never been my favorite swimming places. On summer weekends, as a kid, I could most likely be found paddling around in a chlorinated country club swimming pool where the matching lounge chairs were carefully placed on the pool's concrete deck. While my sisters and I slathered on Coppertone or baby oil to darken our skin with that special summer tan, my mother played bridge or clicked the ivory tiles of mah-jongg with her girlfriends. My father played golf on the club's eighteen-hole links.

Our pool had a snack bar, where we ordered memorably delicious hamburgers and fries or Drumstick ice cream cones that we lapped up from their paper wrappers before they dripped down to our elbows in the clean summer sun. On the hottest days, a truck would back into the pool area and drop a huge block of shimmering ice into the water. I thought that was the way all swimming pools stayed cold against the humidity and summer heat of Central Pennsylvania. I've never again seen or heard of such a practice.

Nevada County is rich with natural bodies of water, many of

which draw from the three forks of the Yuba River. It's the uncertain footing of these natural wonders that makes me fearful. But despite Oregon Creek's sandy and sometimes slimy creek bed, I have to confess that I find this place storybook magical. Particularly very early in the morning when there are few others here. The cloudless sky is picture-perfect and the sun ripples across water that is Coke-bottle green. Dozens of three-inch-long dragonflies searching for mates swoop high overhead.

On any given day, you can also be sure to witness a smattering of mankind that I am unaccustomed to. Today my attention is drawn to an oversized picnic tent occupied by several bearded young men. Their swimsuits are riding low under their big bellies and just low enough behind to reveal their butt cracks. They are smoking weed and murmuring in quiet conversation with one another. It's nine o'clock in the morning and upward of eighty degrees and they've built a fire at the peak of fire season. Surely there must be signs somewhere that wood-burning fires are not permitted here. I don't think they're permitted anywhere in California right now. But these men seem to think they have a right and a need to build a fire. And build they do.

Across the water, little girls with matted hair sport hot pink and chartreuse water wings. They're swinging into the creek from a long rope in a tree whose upper branches are brittle and dry. A lone middle-aged woman floats by with a cigarette hanging from her lips. The smells of weed and cigarettes and the porta-potties up the hill are almost enough to make me want to go home. But I don't. Because aside from the refreshment of these cool waters on the hottest of days, there are lessons here for me to learn.

The toughest lessons are those that teach me to reflect on my natural inclination to be judgmental. The people who come here for the most part are not people like me. Today, we're the only septuagenarians wearing sun shirts to protect us from the cancer-causing ozone. And while my mind is busy thinking about the others here, I can't help but wonder what they are thinking about us. If they care that I look different from them or voted for someone they voted against or got vaccinated against COVID when many of them did not. Or did they? These are things I can't know. And their murmured conversations? What are they talking about? Jerry and I are talking about how to take the best iPhone photos of the water. I'm thinking about what to have for lunch and dinner and asking myself how I ended up in this place with so many people who don't seem to be at all like me.

As I float in this cool water with my straw hat protecting my eyes from the bright sun, I'm also thinking about the judge's response to Freddy Burton's petition. I'm still mystified at how she could have reduced six days of testimony and a man's life to two words: *untimely* and *meritless*. In her defense, the word *untimely* may have referred to the legality of the time bars that restrict how long one can bring new evidence in their case to the courts. But I would argue that the rules of time bars are misguided at best and should be changed.

Untimely in America in 2021? When the subject of racism and mass incarceration is on the lips and minds of so many? Freddy Burton's story couldn't be more timely. But most troubling to me was the judge's deliberate choice of the word *meritless*. Even if the judge didn't find Freddy's version of the story to be true, none of it was meritless. His life wasn't and isn't meritless. And if that is legal jargon, it needs to be changed too.

"I wanted to know from the man himself," George Floyd's brother said to Derek Chauvin as he mopped tears from his eyes at Chauvin's sentencing hearing. "Why? What were you thinking? What was going through your head when you had your knee on my brother's neck? When you knew that he posed no threat anymore. He was handcuffed. Why didn't you at least get up?"

It's what we all wanted to know.

I'd deliberately not watched Chauvin's trial last spring. With the fear of COVID raging, I couldn't handle one more disappointment or listen to one more narrative about how and why it might have been OK for Chauvin to do what he did. If convicted, he would have been one of few white police officers found guilty of crimes in which Black men and women were murdered. I simply couldn't watch it.

But on the day of his sentencing hearing, I found myself glued to my laptop screen. I was hoping that a stiff prison sentence might somehow compensate the Floyd family and the world for Chauvin's cruel and terrifying and very public murder of another human being. Watching that hearing, anger burned in the back of my throat. My worst fear was that I might witness another travesty of justice. That Chauvin would get off easier than Freddy did.

But Derek Chauvin's twenty-two-and-a-half-year prison sentence felt like an eye for an eye to me, with two important exceptions: Chauvin, if he survives, will be out of prison in fifteen years for a crime there is no doubt that he committed. Freddy Burton will more than likely die in prison for crimes that he may not have committed. I can't help but wonder what the different-from-us swimmers at Oregon Creek might think about Derek Chauvin and what he did and how he has been punished. Do they even care?

It's a curse. My morbid curiosity about others who don't look like me. It's in conditioning and genes I can't erase. All I can do is consciously mediate them. But I will always wonder who these "others" are and what they think and why they do what they sometimes do. Should I fear them or reach out to them or scorn them? Or should I not even care?

XXXI
Marbles

As kids, my sister Sue and I collected marbles. I have no memory of how we got started or when the fascination ended. But I remember them being fun to play with and beautiful to look at. On warm summer afternoons, on the four concrete steps behind our house, Sue and I dumped our pouches of marbles onto separate dinner plates and lifted each to the sunlight as a jeweler with a loupe might examine a precious gemstone for clarity and flaws. We sorted them by size, by color, and by the intricate patterns that made them unique.

My favorite marbles were the clear, unblemished glass ones with a wispy filament of color swirled through the center like a thin squeeze of toothpaste. Cat's eyes. When I rolled one of them between my fingers in the summer sun, I imagined meeting the gaze of a bright-eyed curious cat. When Sue and I traded with each other, the cat's eyes were the gems I wanted, even if it meant trading one of the bigger, can't-miss shooter marbles. Then I would line up my treasures by color and let the sun reflect their simple, honest transparency.

I've thought a lot about those cat's eye marbles as I've sifted and sorted the details that led me to write this story. I had so hoped to uncover a single flawless narrative about what happened to Freddy

Burton and how things might have been different. About how and why I made the choice I did to convict him. A narrative as pure and uncomplicated as I remember those simple spheres of glass were.

Instead, I uncovered something messy. Something really messy. What I uncovered were the marbles with nicks and scrapes and chinks in them that made them all less than perfect. The marbles no one wanted. The marbles no one would trade for. Multiple narratives, any one of which could be held forth as true. And I uncovered that this story is about much more than me. Instead, it is about how each and every one of us sees the world through our own single-vision lens. If you've ever tried looking through someone else's eyeglasses, you'll know that what you see is never perfectly clear.

By the time our paths crossed in that city hall courtroom forty-four years ago, Freddy Burton's lot was cast. He was a Black man serving a life sentence for the murder of a white police officer and was on trial for the murders of two white prison wardens.

Whatever Freddy Burton did or didn't do, I feel certain he was not served well by our criminal justice system. Not in his first conviction in 1972. Not in his second in 1976. And not in his Post-Conviction Relief Act hearing in 2020.

In the Von Colln case, he was not served well by a culture in which Frank Rizzo's brutish police force treated him and his community as less than human. He was not served well by that same police force that coerced a frightened Marie Williams to name him as a conspirator. He was not served well by a prosecuting attorney who may have cared more about another notch in his belt for convicting a Black revolutionary than about the truth. He was not served well when the courtroom was cleared of his family members who were present to bear witness. He was not served well by a legal system that allowed an all-white jury to pass judgment on a Black man. And he was not served well when Marie Williams's false statements to the police held sway over character witnesses who testified that Freddy Burton was not the kind of man who would commit that kind of crime. Then he was sentenced to life without parole in a prison where violence not only was tolerated but, some say, was encouraged by the prison administration.

In the Fromhold-Curran case on which I served as a juror, the story is scarcely different. Freddy Burton was not served well by a grandstanding defense attorney who was chastised by the judge for coming to court with alcohol on his breath and then not removed from the case. He was not served well by the twenty-one-day sequestration of a dozen people, many of whom, including me, would have done anything to be somewhere else, doing something else. He was not served well by the law as I heard Judge Prattis explain it to the jury. And finally, he was not served well by me—a young woman whose sheltered life and white privilege gave her no single tool to fairly decide his fate.

And as for his hearing last summer, I am at a loss for words to understand the dispassionate blunt force of the judge's ruling. After six days of legal haranguing, six days of struggling with faulty Zoom connections, and hundreds of pages of transcripts, in her eyes and in the eyes of the law, Freddy Burton's life was summed up in two words: *untimely* and *meritless.* I expected so much more.

It turns out that my friend and fellow juror Alene was the wisest and most prescient of all of us. Freddy Burton was a man who was never going home.

What happened to Freddy Burton and thousands of other Black men in the 1970s and beyond is the product of a four-hundred-year-old flawed system of unequal justice that survives because people with the privilege of being white in America have knowingly and unknowingly failed to see it and failed to change it. People like me at twenty-four years old who cared more about the inconvenience of my sequestration than the life that Freddy Burton lived and the limited choices that circumstances left him.

If you are a gentle reader, you can see that in so many ways, Freddy Burton's story is George Floyd's story and Breonna Taylor's story and Philando Castile's story and Ahmaud Arbery's story and the stories of all the people of color who have had their lives stripped away by the laws and institutions of our country that are long overdue for change. Laws and institutions that perceive people of color as something less than human and protect those who abuse them.

I am no scholar on the subjects of institutional racism, the law, or white privilege. I only know what I know from holding my story up to the light and seeing something far less than perfect.

In 1974, Frederick Burton's attorney, Cecil Moore, told a *Philadelphia Inquirer* reporter, "I say, to hell with the club, let's fight the damn system, I don't want no more than the white man got, but I won't take no less."

XXXII
Coda

In January of 2022, I received this message from Jonathan after the Superior Court of Pennsylvania dismissed Freddy Burton's latest Post-Conviction Relief Act petition:

"I had a wonderful experience with Muhammed (*sic* Freddy) the other day," he wrote. "Our first Zoom call. I took it on my phone. I first showed him our house and our street in Santa Cruz. I then put him in the windshield of the car at sunrise so he could be part of that experience. We drove down to the ocean and watched the sunrise to the East and moon set to the West. We watched surfers, otters, birds and seals. It was a mind-blowing experience for both of us. And I realized that in the time it takes me to get him out of jail physically, I can start chipping away at the prison in both of our minds piece by piece. I can't wait to take him to the redwoods and all over. I thought you would like to carry that image of him experiencing all that beauty in real time even if only through the screen. We may all be downloaded into a virtual reality at some point anyway but our connections will always persist if we develop them meaningfully."

Author's Notes

I recently talked with a stone mason who shared his process for building the sturdiest, most long-lasting stone walls. He does it, he told me, by carefully selecting the right size and shape of each stone and then capping the wall with sturdy, long flat rocks to hold it in place. The telling of my story of being sequestered on a jury for twenty-one days in a dramatic murder trial is like the building of that mason's walls. My stones have been my memories of growing up in the 1950s and 1960s isolated in a world of Jewishness and white privilege, of my coming-of-age in the 1970s, and of growing old in the twenty-first century. My stones have been the memories of my jury service in the Holmesburg Prison-murder trial in 1976. My stones have been newspaper accounts of both crimes Freddy Burton was convicted of and the times in which they took place. And among my stones are those of my imagination about some of the people and events of those times. The most precious stones though—those that cap this story—are the Gettleman family's unrelenting efforts to free Freddy Burton.

Freddy Burton and I have spoken only briefly on the phone one time. I have spoken to his son only twice. When I spoke to Mr. Burton three years ago, he knew I had served on the jury for the prison murders and knew I was trying to help strengthen Jonathan's case on his behalf. In that conversation, I recall saying to him, "I don't know what to say to you." He replied simply, "Well, we are here, aren't we?" It is the conversation I put in my dream of the Florida Keys.

In every way I can, I have attempted to be transparent about what I've written that is from my memory, from my research, or from my imagination. It has all come together in my heart.

I have no doubt that others' stories of the same events will differ from mine. But this is the closest I can come to my truth about my jury service and the way my eyes have been opened to the systemic racism so embedded in America's institutions.

I am grateful to the folks at Temple University's Special Collections Research Center and the local Nevada County librarian for pulling dozens of newspaper articles from microfiche for me. There was a very nice young man at the City of Philadelphia Court of Appeals archives who has tried more than once to find the trial transcripts of both of Freddy's trials. I would have given anything to read the judge's instructions to the jury again. Or to see my letter to Judge Prattis during that twenty-one-day ordeal of sequestration and trial. The file box is there, the young man has told me, but the items I want seem to have disappeared. Some kinder than I am have said it's because of sloppy record-keeping. It was almost fifty years ago, they say. I'm skeptical. I think they've disappeared at the hands of someone who didn't want them found.

I am also grateful to many others who have traveled on this long journey with me. To my partner, Jerry Thomas. To my dear friends Teddi Williams and her daughter Elle Cabot, Carolyn Crane, Diane Arnell, and Mag Diamond, all of whom always seem to get it right. To Sean Murphy and Tania Casselle, whose *Write to the Finish* workshop kept me on task. To the unconditional encouragement from my *Write to the Finish* home team members, again Mag and Deb and Wayne. And to all my friends who never stopped asking how my book was coming. I couldn't have completed this project without them.

And finally, I also feel deep gratitude to those who have helped me along the way to understand what it means to be white in America and, for better or worse, the privileges it affords: Bryan Stevenson and the Equal Justice Initiative's Legacy Museum and National Memorial for Peace and Justice in Montgomery, Alabama; three generations of the Gettleman family; Freddy Burton Jr.; and last but not least, Frederick Muhammed Burton himself. May he one day be set free.

As we neared the publication date for this book, I turned over yet another stone in the quarry of my story. Though still implausible to me, Judge Prattis's instructions to the jury were in fact correct. Under Pennsylvania law, prosecutors can bring a charge of felony murder, also known in the state as second-degree murder, against someone involved in a crime that led to a death. The charge comes with a mandatory sentence of life without parole. This is the law that guided my decision to convict Mr. Burton. More than one thousand people are serving life without parole in Pennsylvania, even though they never intended to kill anyone. Seventy percent of those people are Black. While judges and prosecutors and jurors are duty bound to defend this law, efforts to modify the law and its mandatory sentence are making their way to the Pennsylvania General Assembly.

About the Author

Photo credit: Kathy Triolo

Carol Menaker is a writer living in the Sierra Foothills in Northern California, where she retired after a forty-plus-year career writing and managing communications for universities and nonprofits. She was raised in a Jewish family in Harrisburg, Pennsylvania. She holds a BA in theatre arts/acting from Pennsylvania State University and an MS in journalism from the University of Illinois at Urbana-Champaign, and she enjoys travel, yoga, walking, and bicycling. *The Worst Thing We've Ever Done* is her first full-length work.

Visit her website at carolmenaker.com.

SELECTED TITLES FROM SHE WRITES PRESS

She Writes Press is an independent publishing company founded to serve women writers everywhere. Visit us at www.shewritespress.com.

Redlined: A Memoir of Race, Change, and Fractured Community in 1960s Chicago by Linda Gartz. $16.95, 978-1-63152-320-5
A riveting story of a community fractured by racial turmoil, an unraveling and conflicted marriage, a daughter's fight for sexual independence, and an up-close, intimate view of the racial and social upheavals of the 1960s.

Hoosier Hysteria: A Fateful Year in the Crosshairs of Race in America by Meri Henriques Vahl. $16.95, 978-1-63152-465-6
Meri Henriques, a naïve freshman from New York, arrives to Indiana University in September of 1963 expecting an idyllic midwestern college experience; instead, she finds herself thrust into the middle of violent political unrest and escalating racial tensions.

In the Game: The Highs and Lows of a Trailblazing Trial Lawyer by Peggy Garrity. $16.95, 978-1-63152-105-8
Admitted to the California State Bar in 1975—when less than 3 percent of lawyers were women—Peggy Garrity refuses to choose between family and profession, and succeeds at both beyond anything she could have imagined.

Life's Hourglass: A Memoir of Chasing Success at a Cost by Janice Mock. $16.95, 978-1-63152-005-5
When Janice Mock's stage four cancer diagnosis causes her to examine her career as a successful trial lawyer and the relentless drive for wealth and excess that corporate America promotes, she comes to the realization that she must change in order to make the most of the rest of her life.

Freedom Lessons by Eileen Harrison Sanchez. $16.95, 978-1-63152-610-7
A heartfelt, unflinching novel about the unexpected effects of school integration in 1960s Louisiana told by three very different people living in the same rural town: Colleen, an idealistic young white teacher; Frank, a black high school football player; and Evelyn, an experienced black teacher.